Cherokee Blue Eyes

Cherokee Blue Eyes

Keeping the Heritage Alive

Brian Voncannon

Writers Club Press
San Jose New York Lincoln Shanghai

Cherokee Blue Eyes
Keeping the Heritage Alive

Writers Club Press
an imprint of iUniverse.com, Inc.

For information address:
iUniverse.com, Inc.
5220 S 16th, Ste. 200
Lincoln, NE 68512
www.iuniverse.com

The opinions contained within are that of the author's and not of any one particular tribal entity. No liability is assumed for any information contained herein.

ISBN: 0-595-15774-2

Printed in the United States of America

Dedication

To my family and all people with Native American heritage, particularly the Ani-Yunwiya (the principal people). Also, a special dedication goes to the Lord Jesus Christ, the true Creator. Without each of these, I would not be here.

Epigraph

Long ago we stood alone, but today we must all stand as one…

The author

Contents

Acknowledgments

The writing of a book is not an easy task. It means being up late and getting up early. You have to give up some personal time that you would normally be doing other things. Although an enjoyable experience, it can be quite challenging. The worry of whether your book is going to be successful is a burden within itself. Without the support of my family during these times, my accomplishments would not be possible. Therefore, I would like to extend a special thanks to my family for putting up with me during my time at the keyboard. Also, a very special thanks goes to Karen, a young lady that is as important to me as the air that I breathe. Thanks for bearing with me during the long hours that I spent making my dreams of becoming an author a reality.

Introduction

I would like to welcome you to another publication of mine. This book is one of several that I have written within the last two years, four of which that have been published. I must say that the one that you hold in your hands is one of my better pieces of work. I spent many hours and put a great deal of heart into it. I am sure that you will draw that conclusion as you read this book.

Obviously, this book deals with Native American heritage and some ideals of mine that go along with it. This is not really a genealogy book, nor a record book. It does contain some research tips in one of the chapters that may aid you in your search. I included this in order to make the point that by being proud enough of your roots to seek them out, you are honoring your ancestors. There are plenty of books out there concerning most tribes that are well known today. If you are still seeking your roots and need records, then I would have to point you elsewhere. However, even in the midst of researching native roots, this text will enlighten you on what you may experience in the mainstream of seeking your Native American connections.

I always like to begin a book with an explanation of it's title. Certainly, the title of this book catches the eye somewhat, and I feel that it deserves some explaining. As I will tell you shortly, this book contains a variety of ideas. The main thrust of the book deals with my views as a mixed blood Native American, namely honoring one's ancestors, and some opinions that concern the history of the nation's first people. The title, *Cherokee Blue Eyes*, was one that I felt would give you the feeling that even though I peer at you through baby blue eyes, my Cherokee blood is still strong.

Obviously, the mention of blue eyes indicates that I am of a mixed background. The subtitle, *Keeping the Heritage Alive*, tells another story in a few short words. This gives you an idea of what I am going to discuss. From the subtitle as well as this introduction, you should see that I am going to give you my views on how a mixed blood Native American can keep the blood strong, even in the face of controversy. Maybe you could look at this book as a struggle for my own heritage to survive.

This book is basically opinionated and many ideas will probably rub some folks the wrong way. I did not write this book, as any of my books, to offend anyone. Although, I have found that no matter what one says, there will always be someone who is just completely devastated. You will find that dealing with Native American research is no exception. This book surrounds that subject and covers some facts that will interest you.

During the course of this book, I will mention many subjects and questions that come up in the minds of those who are seeking to establish their roots with one tribe or another. Some you may not like, and some you may find amusing. No matter which emotion that this book sparks within you, I feel that you will enjoy the reading. The key is to keep an open mind and read it from front to back. It will make much better sense that way. My style of writing is a bit different from others, but that is what makes us as unique as each single snowflake that falls during a winter storm.

How I put this book together is actually an interesting story within itself. I originally had published a great deal of it on the Internet about a year ago on my heritage web page. This was in the form of an essay entitled *The Story of Me and Other Things: A Rather Large Essay Concerning Indian Ancestry Outside The Reservations, The "Wannabe" Syndrome, and Other Things That Cause Allergic Reactions.* This site was located at http://members.tripod.com/~vcassociates/wannabe.html. I received a great deal of interest in this essay, as well as many kind comments surrounding the same. In response to that interest, I felt that a book would be in order. Although I had to remove the essay due to publication policies of my publisher, the site is still there and discusses the book.

The essay that inspired this book was definitely one of my better expressions of myself. I have to admit that I was a bit agitated when I wrote the original essay. When I am angry, I tend to use very humorous adjectives to describe my feelings. Why was I angry? You will find out as you read the chapter that contains the essay mentioned above. I think that you will understand. If not, then I hope you enjoy my humorous way of expressing myself.

The concept of this book does not particularly apply to any one tribe. Although using my Cherokee heritage as an example, this book does not reflect the opinions of the Cherokee Nation, or any one tribal entity mentioned within this text, and I do not claim to officially represent them in any way. This book is purely my opinion, and I speak totally from my own standpoint. I may mention different tribes and organizations throughout the book, but just keep in mind that these are only examples. As in the original essay, I ask you to respect my views, and I will respect yours to the best of my ability.

The other parts of this book are quite diverse, but all have a common purpose of honoring one's ancestors. Although the essay that I wrote concerning Indian ancestry outside of the reservations inspired the meat of this book, the other subjects go together quite nicely. I have included some reprinted information from a few books that I self-published some time ago that I thought would be a good addition to this work. The chapter entitled *Honoring Your Ancestors* contains much of this information. Keep in mind that this book is not a how-to book concerning being Indian. I will state it many times in this book, but it is the truth. There is no such volume available. You either are or you are not. Maybe we could say that being Indian is simply being.

I want to explain some terminology used in this book up front. Throughout the book's entirety, I interchange the words Indian, Native American, Mixed blood, Native, etc. I have heard some say that the word

Indian was offensive to them. Some prefer to be called Indian, while others prefer to be called Native American. Many do not care which. I guess that I fall into the latter. Truthfully, before the white man arrived, no one was an Indian. They were simply human beings. After time progressed, a label was placed upon their heads. Sometimes I am not sure that the label has ever come off. In any rate, my intentions are not to offend anyone by the terminology that I use. I simply use the words to properly illustrate my point and to acquaint you with what is out there today.

I always explain to people that I receive no monetary gain from my heritage nor my tribal membership. I work just like everyone else and have never asked for any money just because I proclaim my heritage proudly. I say this because I have been accused of the same, if you can believe it. I will go deeper into that subject as the book progresses, so I will not try to explain at this point. I feel that the problem is that in our modern day, we all seem to want something. Very few today will do something nice for you or be proud of something unless there is pay back. Maybe we have gotten so busy that we have forgotten to just do something good without needing to receive something in return. I will tell you that in the Native American circuit, I have met many who still do though. It was told to me that when you have something good, you are to share it with others. If that is an *old school* idea, maybe it isn't such a bad thing to say that old ways are sometime the best ways.

Once again, I welcome you to this book and I hope that those of you that have mixed native roots will enjoy my thoughts that come straight from the heart. The book is full of a variety of thoughts and information, but I feel that it will answer many of your questions. I feel that this is something good. This is the story of me.

Chapter One

Mixed Blood

From reading the title of this book, as well as the introduction, you can see that it is written by one of a mixed European/Native American background. This entire book is presented from my own point of view as the introduction has told you. Probably, there will be parts in this book that some of you may disagree with. That is okay. This is America, and we do have the freedom to think as an individual. That is one of the reasons that I wrote this book. Most of my writings are based on factual events or history. In the past, I have written family history books that included a twist of Native American background, and I have written a book about my experiences as a law enforcement officer. The one that you hold in your hands is similar in nature to my first two, but yet totally unique in it's own way.

During this book, I will take you on a journey through various subjects that all relate to Native American heritage. In all of these subject areas, it is from a mixed blood standpoint. What makes that different? Well, that question could be answered many different ways. Maybe I should clarify the fact that I am speaking from a mixed blood that did not grow up on an Indian reservation. That definitely could change my views on certain issues, or maybe it shouldn't. I am sure that you are aware of the problems that reservation inhabitants face today. If you are not, I can tell you that there are problems there just as there are problems outside of the bound-aries. I must state that I cannot speak from an expert point of view on such a topic since I did not grow up on a reservation. My neighbor's grandmother grew up on the Cherokee Indian Reservation and I am sure that he could attest to the economic challenges that were faced there.

I spend quite a bit of time at the Cherokee Indian Reservation in North Carolina. I love the Smoky Mountains and look forward to returning each and every time. I will go into that later. For now, I just wanted to enlighten you about the reservation if you are unfamiliar. From the average citizen's view point, you would probably see the reservation as a vacation spot with lots to do with your family. This is a fact. I can tell you that there are some wonderful things to see and do in Cherokee that the whole family would enjoy. Other than the beauty of the Great Smoky Mountains, this may be the extent of what you see. After all, most go there for a vacation or to visit the infamous Harrah's Cherokee Casino.

Now, let me explain what I see. Sure, I see the same things that you do. I see the mountains, the entertainment, and the tourists. All of these things are important for both the visitor and for the Eastern Band of Cherokee Indians. Since the opening of the parkway, the tourist industry has become a livelihood for the Band. Above and beyond these attributes, I see some more important things.

I see a proud people that have endured hardship for many generations. I see a quiet struggle for survival going on within the Band. I see ambitious young people that are seeking a chance to become what that want to be. I see people who are both average and economically challenged. Most importantly, I see a large group of people bound to me by blood ties, living within the arms of the sleeping giants that are called the Great Smoky Mountains. I guess that you could say that I get an eye full each time that I return to the area!

As I stated earlier, should my views of the above be any different if I had grown up on the Qualla Boundary? Maybe they would and maybe they would not. That question cannot truthfully be answered from my standpoint due to that fact that I did not grow up there. Even so, I am still very receptive to what I perceive in the environment that I am in. I try to allow all of the feelings to flow into my head naturally as they come. I must say that I enjoy gaining new insight and learning more about the Cherokee each time that I visit them.

If I have confused you thus far, do not put the book down yet! The essence of my statements in this chapter is leading up to the feelings that I have for my heritage. I have heard non-reservation mixed bloods put down by many people. Often times, the words are *selling out to white culture*, and *your family just couldn't stick it out with us.* Although such statements could be taken harshly, I do not become angry when someone makes such a statement to me. I understand their anger, and I can see that their lives probably were harder than those that managed to start a new life away from the tribe. No matter who says they did not, there were plenty of families that did. It is here that the heritage begins to become lost or hidden within families.

In my own views, I feel that there will probably always be some that will harbor ill feelings towards those that grew up away from the tribe. I know that not all think this way, but some do. That may never change and there is probably little that I could say or do to change their minds. Another view that I have on this is the fact that no matter what is thought of me, I will always be proud of who I am and who my ancestors were. Those feeling can never be changed either. Should I be ridiculed for such a way of thinking?

Within the United States, there are many people that have some Native American blood in their veins. Whether it be Cherokee, Sioux, Creek, or any other tribe, the roots are there. Many of these are completely unaware that they descend from such people. What a great pride they are being deprived of by not knowing who they are! Then there are those who know of their heritage, but do not really care or simply are ashamed of it for one reason or another. I can't see being ashamed of it, but there are still those who are. This goes way back to the days when it was practically illegal to be an Indian in a white man's world. I have heard these very statements made by some of my own older relatives in the past. Sadly, I had some relatives that rebuked my other family members when they mentioned our Cherokee blood. You see, it didn't matter whether you were a full blood or not. Years ago, an Indian was an Indian, not matter how minute the blood. You may find that hard to believe today. Believe me, it went a whole lot deeper than that. If you knew of only half of the wrongs that were done to all Native American tribes, it would turn your stomach.

I guess that I am trying to make the point that if you are a lonely mixed blood in a white man's world, your views of your heritage are a personal choice. In other words, you can choose to be proud of who you are and enjoy the pride of being Native American, even though you are not a full blood. You can revive the culture and pass your findings down to your children so that the heritage is not lost. On the other hand, you can be like some mentioned above, and simply ignore it or be ashamed. I have a problem with that, but some evidently do not. I guess that is their choice.

By the way, how much blood does it take to make one Cherokee? Would it be one half, one quarter, or even less? Better yet, to whom do I direct this question? Should I ask the Bureau of Indian Affairs, the tribe, or my family? Who can tell me who I really am? Granted, there have been many people that I didn't know who wanted to tell me who I was. It is not that I didn't appreciate them trying to set me straight, but you could say that their comments are now stored in the four-sided vertical file. In my opinion, your family is the only one who can tell you who you really are. You might not be accepted by the others, but who really matters to you? You will have to answer that one yourself.

I have had some folks ask me what I get out of being proud about my lineage. Some just can't seem to figure out why I would *waste* my time with something that wasn't going to make me a pile of money. It angers me to hear words as these, but they have been said to me before. My answer to them is usually an explanation of how many of the problems today encircle just that. We just don't think that anything is worthwhile unless it yields a monetary return. I then go on to explain how there are some things in this world that are worth more than money. If you get down to it, maybe the introduction of the inequality of wealth into the Cherokee society was actually a downfall. It is the same outside of the tribe.

I like to tell people that I am an old fashion kind of guy. They sometimes look at me with one eyebrow raised as if I am a nut. I realize that I am only 31 years old, but I was raised by old principles. Even I am guilty of saying that *things just aren't the way they used to be.* Is this a sign of becoming wiser or just getting old? Many who are non-Indian often wonder if I follow the old native ways when I make such a statement. My response to that usually involves me stating that if respecting your elders, being mindful of other's feelings, and not being afraid to help others falls into that category, then yes I do.

You may be asking why I have included thoughts such as those in the proceeding paragraphs in a book about being a mixed blood Native American. That answer is simple. I am human. Television and other forms of modern media have painted a picture in the world's mind that an Indian is some type of savage. Although these methods of entertainment usually focus during the early days of American history, people still stereotype Native Americans to be holding onto some type of savagery or an inhuman way of living. I realize that this sounds completely nuts, but you might be surprised how much truth there is to this statement. Maybe this is why so many people don't actually believe you when you tell them that you are of Native heritage. They tend to fall back on that television stereotype, whether consciously or unconsciously, and figure that you could not be telling the truth. I have met countless people who thought that I was making up some kind of lie to impress people.

One of the biggest excuses that I heard from one of these people that thought I was full of it, was the fact that I live three hours east of the Cherokee domain. Wow, what a reason. They are right, there is no possible way that a Cherokee could wonder that far. After all, they are not people, or capable of making decisions on their own right? Absolutely wrong. Of course, I still don't bother to argue with them and go into my spill on how my grandma's people were from the mountains of Tennessee, Georgia, Alabama, and out west. I simply grind my teeth, swallow the anger, and walk away. I think that this is where I get the most aggravated.

Here again, I don't feel that I have to prove my family tree to strangers, nor do I need to whip out my enrollment card and ask for their approval. Just be prepared for such types of people if you decide to be public with who you are.

As you proceed through this book, you will learn exactly how I honor my heritage and what I think of that heritage. By now, you should have a good idea. Although a minute few of my relatives scolded my grandmother and others from talking about our Cherokee blood, the rest taught me to be proud of it. I have chosen that path to follow. Whether I am accepted by my Cherokee brothers and sisters or not, my pride will never change. Could it be that people such as I only make the Nation stronger? I am but one person and do not consider myself to be of any importance. However, just like the inside of a clock, the small wheels help keep the big ones moving!

I do not discount my other ancestral ties. Since I am not a full blood Cherokee, I obviously have other blood ties within my family. From English to Saponi Indian, I am one big melting pot. Even though I acknowledge these other bloods, it has always been that my Cherokee heritage has spoken louder than any other connection that I have. I have to tell you that I thank God for all of my ancestors, as I would not be here without them! I can't say that I agree with everything that some of them did, but I am still related to them.

As I come to the close of this short chapter, I want to summarize what I was trying to portray to you. I wanted you to see that even one who did not grow up on a reservation or posses pure Cherokee blood could still see things that some may think that I could not. I wanted you to see that I can feel more than just a statement of how I am a mixed blood descendant of a proud people. It is my hopes that my readers and all that know me, will understand that I truly care for my ancestors. It is important to me and I am not ashamed. Even in the face of ridicule, I have stayed headstrong or maybe stubborn would be a better word!

I also wanted you to understand that it is not necessarily the amount of blood that flows in your veins which determines who you are. I have seen people who were less than 1/256th Cherokee that had a deeper love for their heritage than some full bloods. I think that it is in the heart and not the veins. Of course, not having a certain amount of Native American blood may keep you from obtaining tribal membership from certain tribes. Just remember that a membership card does not make the person. We have probably all used the term *part Indian*. This falls back onto what we have just discussed. You can say that you are part this or that, but which part of you belongs to what? If you must say that you are part Indian, then I would tell people that the part of me that is Indian is my heart.

You should also conclude through this chapter that Native Americans are real people. Forget the television stereotypes and just accept them as fellow human beings. You have also seen that I too am human. I have opinions just like everyone else. What makes me different is the fact that I have my own special way for viewing my heritage. You will see that more and more as the book goes on. We also discussed how there are certain types of people that are completely convinced that unless you speak broken English or have long black hair, you cannot have any Indian heritage. If I park a Teepee in my backyard, would it help any? All I really want is for you to respect the First People and to see the Cherokee in me, while gazing past my blue eyes.

Chapter Two

Why Search for Native Roots?

You may ask a question such as the title of this section. Many people search for their ancestry for many reasons, but today, searching for Native American heritage has become a big business. I did not know that there was such an influx of people trying to establish their Indian identity until I got into my research project. Actually, I did not know that most even cared for that part of their past unless they were full blood. Let me stop here and explain a few terms before I go any further so that you will better understand what I mean throughout the book.

You will see several words in this book such as, mixed blood, full blood, part blood, blood quantum, government rolls, Eastern Band, and the Cherokee Nation West. Each of these words have significance in this book as well as when you are dealing with any Native American research project. The blood terms listed above deal with those either of pure Indian ancestry or those who are of European and Indian descent. The term *blood quantum* is a word basically coined by Uncle Sam to explain how much Indian blood one has in his or her veins. I will get into that subject later, but for now, that is what it means.

The government rolls are a group of census lists taken by the federal governments years ago that were used to account for the Indians in a particular area or for the purpose of removal, land allotments, or payment. These too will be explained to you later on in the book. The term *Eastern Band* refers to the Cherokees which reside in the mountains of North Carolina. This area is also called the Qualla Boundary or the Cherokee Indian Reservation. The *Cherokee Nation West* refers to the main body of Cherokee which reside in Oklahoma. This group of Cherokees, which numbers well over 150,000, is the result of the infamous trail of tears and the land that the government put them on. This one will require a good bit of explaining later on also.

Now that I have explained the above, we can proceed with this section with a better understanding. As I was saying, many people have begun their search for their native beginnings. I guess that I could be speculating on why such a recent interest, but I feel that there are several reasons. Some of the reasons may be unfavorable and most are out of pure pride in who they are. I would hope that by now, you know which category that I fit into! Okay, here is what I have run across during the course of my research. I found, in some rare cases, that many seek to establish their heritage for the purpose of benefits in the form of money, college, or profession. That sounds pretty bad without any explanation so far, huh? The others are those like myself, who are proud of who they are and only wish to honor their ancestors and revive a heritage that may have been hidden for one reason or another. Let's talk about the bad reasons first.

I know that it sounds bad, but I have spoken to people who were wanting to claim their heritage for the mere purpose of personal gain. I guess that this is one reason why many mixed bloods who did not grow up in the tribal area are frowned upon. Life on the reservation is not all fun and games. From day one, the Cherokee people have had many troubles since the white man entered their lives. They were pushed off of their lands, killed, enslaved, and denied equality among the population for a long time. They do not receive large payments from the government just because they live on a reservation. They have troubles just like anyone else. I have been told that some mixed bloods are sometimes frowned upon because they left the tribe and "sold out" their heritage for a better way of life. I do not harbor any bad feelings towards any of my Indian brothers or sisters, but I don't feel that my family had such a goal in mind. Most may call it a goal of survival and seeking a better way of existence for their children. I will cover that topic to my specific family later on.

Anyway, many have sought money for their heritage. Unfortunately, most of these are mixed bloods who did not grow up on the reservation and may have not known of their past until someone told them. They then start their search for the purpose of getting *some of that government money* as I have heard it explained. I have personally heard people say that they only wanted to establish their heritage for that purpose. Let me say that I do not feel there is anything wrong with any assistance that the Indian people get from Uncle Sam. Many of our brothers and sisters on the reservations are in need just as there are those outside of the boundary that need help. When you learn more of their history, you will understand where I am coming from.

I have been personally accused of establishing my heritage because I wanted something. There are those who know me that think I am getting some type of money or land from my lineage. They actually think that is all that I care about. I take that as an insult to myself, my family, my ancestors, and the Cherokee people. Besides the fact that there is no such thing as an *Indian check*, I receive nothing from the government nor anyone else for that matter. I do what I do and I am who I am for one reason alone, and that is to honor my ancestors. I am proud of who my family is and I enjoy learning all that I can about them and where they came from….period! Those that do otherwise are merely the bad seeds in the bunch that make it hard on the rest of us who have a heart pure enough to be tried by fire. Of course, it does not stop there.

I have run into another group of people whom I still find a bit intrusive. This group of people are those who have no Indian blood at all, but seek either to establish a false identity or to adopt Indian culture. Some may argue with me over this point, but since I have been publishing books, I am used to that idea. I have been told that there were those who fabricated Indian heritage because they felt guilty about what their ancestors had done to the Indians. I don't know about that idea. That sounds like it takes too much effort and conscience for someone to be that way and quite frankly, I haven't met anyone like that too often today. That could have been the case after the removal with someone who actually took part in the act and had a strong feeling of guilt, but for someone to make it up today, I just don't feel it is a likely reason. The next area in this subject seems to fall within what is known today as the *new age movement.* This stirs up quite a bit in the realm of Native America.

I do not the follow the new age movement, but I am somewhat familiar with it. The new age movement could be considered a religion, so I will try to make my point without overstepping my bounds and upset someone as to think that I am trying to violate their freedom of religion. I will tell you up front that I am a born again Christian of the Southern Baptist faith and will always be. I gave my heart to Jesus when I was eight years old and he has never left me. The new age movement takes on many forms and many of those forms comes from Indian culture. There seems to be an increasing interest in angels, crystal power, pyramids, and items of traditional Indian culture. Keep in mind that many of the items that are commonly sought after in the new age movement are of Indian background. One such object is the crystal. The crystal was a sacred object to the Cherokee and to other tribes to a lesser degree. It was thought to possess power in the form of healing as well as spirituality. Other objects such as the dream catcher, herbs, and certain gem stones are all of native origin in the area of religious practice. It is these items that I speak of that have been incorporated into other cultures.

I am not saying that it is wrong for people of European or other backgrounds to adopt Indian culture or practices. I am just saying that sometimes the origins are not stated and people start to associate these things with groups of people that many call cults or strange. Then, when they see a Native American wearing a crystal about his neck or see a dream catcher hanging in his bedroom, they think that this person belongs to some weird group of people. I know that everyone who uses these objects are not Satanists or strange people, but some of the general population may think so. This is especially true when the proper respect to the origins of the item or practices is not proclaimed. If these groups wish to adopt native culture and use it for personal development, then that is their choice. They should just make it known where the culture came from and respect it. The other problem is having the general population understand that. Maybe the cultures should not cross in certain situations to avoid more stereotypes or maybe there should not be a use of Indian culture outside of Native Americans at all. If you think that I am the only one who thinks this way, try asking the *American Indian Movement (A.I.M.)* what they think about new agers. I believe that you will get a strong answer!

I know that I am probably stepping on some toes here, but I am just reporting what I have heard people say. I just don't want someone thinking that because I have a medicine bag, that I am an evil witch or some type of alien. Anyway, these things should be kept to yourself and are not for show in any rate. So the bottom line is that many may see these groups and feel that they are the Indians and whatever they do, that is the way it was. Some of these people may fabricate an Indian heritage to make their acquaintances think that they are more "enlightened" or something. I just am not sure what is going on there. The moral of the story is just give respect where it is due.

The lighter side of this is that the settlers did learn quite a bit from our ancestors and we all follow many of those ideals today whether we know it or not. The settlers received information and instruction on medicine, farming, hunting, building homes, and survival from our ancestors at the first contact. Have the Indians been properly repaid for such a contribution? Well, enslavement, theft of land, and murder do not seem like what I would call thanks back in the old days or today either. Think about it, the settlers came over and were given these things and in return, wanted more.

As a matter of fact, they wanted it all. The white man's greed and the fever of gold made the Cherokee nation and other tribes bleed. I realize that I am part European descent and I cannot help that. I do not agree with what the settlers did and can do nothing to change history, but I can be proud of my Indian heritage. No, I am not feeling guilty and making up a false Indian heritage, I am Native American and proud of it. Those that did push our people off of their lands are dead and gone. I do not hold a chip on my shoulder, but I haven't forgotten either. I am also not going to say that the problems are over either. There are still things today that are not right and not fair to our people. I will not go into that as it would require another volume.

Okay, now we have covered most of the main reasons people search for their native roots. There could be others and that's fine, but I feel that this is the majority. Please understand that most are proud of who they are and not everyone is seeking gain from such a heritage. I just had to make you aware of what is out there. There is always a few people who make it difficult on the rest and it will always be that way. Whatever reason you choose, just keep in mind who your ancestors were and respect them. If you do not keep your heritage alive, it may die and your future generations will never know where they came from or the battles that were fought to allow them to be here.

The next section is sort of a diary of how I came to appreciate my heritage and the pathways that I traveled to get there. My pride nor my research are not complete and probably never will be. The research of a family history is never one hundred percent complete, until you can trace back to Adam and Eve!! Obviously, that would be quite impossible, but it is the truth. There are many ways today to research family lineage including DNA testing and other scientific methods. I read a section in a book the other day that stated that after much DNA testing, scientists found that North and South American Indians have Oriental DNA. In other words, that proves the fact that they came from the East and traveled across the Bering Straight to where they are today. Still, the history is shrouded in a mist of time, but is slowly coming into light. This book is one more piece to the beginning of what has already been written in time.

As promised, I will cover more on research later, but for now we will discuss how I was told of my heritage and who I am. These could be some very long chapters, as I see myself as very complex and diverse. I assure you that I will not bore you with unnessesary garble in the next couple of chapters! It is important that I tell you how the fire in my heart was started. You may find that the story sounds all too familiar to you too.

Chapter Three

The Spark that Started the Fire

I felt that I could not complete this book without giving you some background on myself and my own quest for my native roots. As I told you earlier, this is not a genealogy book. However, it is important that I use my own heritage as an example to get my points across to you. You will find that my story may be very similar to yours. After all, aren't we all related somehow? These next chapters deal with the search for my roots and what inspired me to do the same.

Ever since I was a small boy, my mother had spoken of our Cherokee heritage. It was a very comfortable conversation for us to have and I accepted it without question. Mom told me how her grandfather Lambert was part Cherokee and how he loved spending time in the mountains. I heard what she and the rest of the family were saying, but it just never sparked any interest as to research my ancestry to find more about where we came from. It wasn't that I did not care, nor did it mean that I did not believe her. I was just young, accepted the fact that I was "part Indian", and went on with my childhood. It wasn't until my adult years that my heritage became an important project of mine. I will say that I was proud of my heritage as a child and spoke of it to my friends in elementary school on several occasions. I just did not know all of the details. That would all change over time.

Does it surprise you today that someone of Native American heritage could not know everything about his heritage from birth up? Does it seem strange that I did not live on an Indian reservation or attend an Indian school? If you are in touch with reality, you will not find that unusual. Of course, many people today think that if the above were not true or if I did not speak broken English, then there is no way that I could have Indian blood in my veins. The fact of the matter is that there are many people in the country with Native American ancestry who do not even know it! Not everyone was Cherokee, but many are of other tribal bloods. In the case of mixed blood families, it is not uncommon for the heritage to be completely lost over time. This occurred for many reasons, but the most prominent being pure fear of discrimination. In the old days, which was not so long ago, Indians were treated pretty much like animals. African Americans were not the only ones to be treated poorly in the past. Did you know that the Indian removal act was not taken off the books until not so long ago? Indians could not vote in the past nor did they have the rights that whites had. So, have the problems really stopped?

In any rate, I still had Cherokee blood in my veins, but lived as white all of my life. On the other hand, maybe I was taught more Natve principles than I thought. The stories were still taught to me and I am who I am. The heritage is the same, but with a different pathway of existence. I grew up on a farm in Midland, North Carolina which is about three hours from the Cherokee Indian reservation in the mountains. Both of these areas are important to me and I feel at home at either place. I lived here in the country, but had a strange home sickness for a land just a few hours up the road. Let me say that my story is probably very common among mixed blood families who live away from the tribal area that they have ancestral ties to. You do not have to live on a reservation to have Indian blood in your past. Your ancestors may have lived there, but you cannot help where your family moved to in the past. The fact is that the lineage is there and will always be.

So up to this point you know that I was aware of my heritage since childhood, accepted the fact, and went on with my life. You know that I did not grow up on the Qualla Boundary or as it is better known, the Cherokee Indian reservation. You know that I am proud of who I am, and so is the rest of my family. Now comes the reason for this book and for everything that has led me up to this point.

As an adult, being of mixed Cherokee ancestry took on a whole new light. They say that as you get older, you will start to appreciate things more and hold things dear to you that once was looked on as something to take for granted. My heritage is no exception. As I became older, my Cherokee ancestry became my whole life. I learned that I had neglected so great a lineage since childhood and regret that I did not start studying my history before adulthood. No, I did not decide to "become Indian" one day. I always have known and always have been Cherokee, but without spending the time honoring my ancestors the way that I should have. I chose to make amends with my ancestors and honor them the best way that I know how. This book is one aspect of that effort and has become a most important part of me and where I came from.

Several years ago, I was attending First Baptist Church of Locust, NC on a Sunday night. We had a guest speaker that night, a Cheyenne Indian woman, who was a missionary. She too was a mixed blood and spent much of her life on their tribal lands as a child. She had dedicated her life to the work of the Lord Jesus Christ and teaching her Indian family about him. She was asked to speak to our church that night and I am glad that I did not miss that service. Anyway, as I listened to what she had to say, something came over me. I heard how proud she was of her heritage and what God had done for her. She spoke of being thankful to God for her heritage and for what he had done for her people. It was that moment that created the spark in the fire of my heritage. It suddenly hit me that I had been neglecting my ancestry. My heart became burdened with the fact that I had let my Cherokee blood slip onto the "back burner" in my life. I was thankful to God for my family and ancestors, it was just that I had not shown it the best that I could have. From that moment on, I vowed that would change. To this day, I have kept the promise and this book is the story of the fire of my heart and the Cherokee people which I call family.

Chapter Four

Who I Am

I am still not through telling you my personal story! This is where it really starts to come together for me as a young man. If you get anything out of the following paragraphs, I think that it will be a better acquaintance with the author this book and an idea of how many come to know of their Native American heritage. Keep in mind that some folks may not find out that they Native American until they are in their elderly years or maybe not at all. I saw a video titled Tracing Your Native American Heritage with Gregg Howard as the narrator. On the video, there was a woman who did not find out that she was Sioux until she was middle aged. That might not sound too hard for you to believe, but the fact that she was actually born on a reservation makes it even more pronounced! If someone can be born on an Indian reservation and have their heritage hidden from them, just imagine how difficult it can be for those that grew up hundreds of miles from their tribes! The moral of this story is that anything is possible and that some genealogists tend to be too quick to tell folks that their heritage is a tissue of lies. With that thought in mind, I will tell you more about how I came to find who I am.

Growing up in North Carolina was a good thing to me. I lived in the country all of my life, except for my short stay in the U.S. Army. As a child, I was reared on a farm and had few friends in my neighborhood, so I spent much time outdoors playing in the woods. It was then that I learned of an unusual love of nature and the animals, which eventually became the majority of my friends. I loved being outside and helped my father on the farm during the summers. I fished with my grandfather, and even hunted some until the age of about 13. After that, hunting seemed to feel wrong to me and my mother taught me that unless I was starving or needed clothes, then hunting was wasteful and considered a crime against the animals. That idea made sense to me and I have not hunted again since.

I went to elementary school at Bethel school through sixth grade. While in school, it is normal for students to study history and the beginnings of our nation. When we got to the section on Indians, I had some questions. At this point, I was about 7 or 8 years old. I remember it well. I came home from school and was talking to my mother about what we were studying in class, which happened to be the trail of tears and the Cherokee. I found the stories fascinating and had an unusual interest in this subject. I hated history for the most part, but this was different. This seemed to hit me pretty hard. To really make this story more understandable to you, I have to tell you a bit more about these feelings prior to me asking my mother. While studying the Indians, I always felt a very comfortable type of feeling. I cannot explain it on paper, but a love of these people and a closeness is the best that I can do. I had been feeling this long before I spoke to my mother about why I felt this way.

Anyway, I came home and talked with mom about the trail of tears and the Cherokee. While we were talking she said it to me for the first time. I can still hear this in my head and it will ring forever. Those words were, "did you know that you are Cherokee?" It really interested me, but I didn't know what to ask next except, "how is that?" Mom then went on to tell me for the first time about her grandfather Lambert. She told me how he was of mixed Cherokee heritage and how he had taught her about that. She told me about how he spent a great deal of time in the mountains and how he had knocked a bear down the mountain with a big stick. This was the first introduction to a man that I had never met, but had no idea that over the course of my life, would come to know him so well. The fire started then, but was only smoldering.

Shortly after that conversation, I remember bragging on my great grandfather Lambert to my friends at school. I remember telling them how I was Cherokee and told them some of the stories about grandpa Lambert that mom had taught me. I did not feel any shame or fear, just a feeling that a missing piece of a puzzle had been found and it fit exactly where I thought it would. I kept up with this pride for a while, then just being a young boy took over and it became a memory, but not lost. If I only knew how important that moment in my life was when I first learned that I was a mixed blood Indian. If I could do it all over again, I would start my research as a child and continue it throughout my life time. You know how kids are, they just don't know the importance of certain things until they get a bit older. I didn't do anything wrong, I was just a kid! I was worried about school, playtime, Christmas, and other normal ideals. I was proud of my heritage, but just didn't know what to do with it yet. Oh, how that would change!!

As I grew older, I kept the memories of my heritage and never forgot. I had lost my grandparents at an early age, so I did not have them around to tell me about those things anymore. My mother, aunts, and uncles were the ones who would teach me what I needed to know. I guess that the section of this book entitled *The Spark that Started the Fire*, should have actually come next, but it doesn't. I will just refer back to that section at this point of my life. That was really when I decided to pursue my heritage and bring it back fully into existence. At this time, I was older, and had begun to understood what it meant to be of Indian ancestry. Anyway, you just about have to be older to truly understand what it means and to enjoy the benefit of knowing about where you came from. I am trying to make up for all of those lost years that I did not pursue the study of my past and make it come alive today more than it ever has. I guess you could say that I am the first since my great grandfather and my mother's generation, to proclaim our heritage as he did to many of our family members. I am very much like him in many ways and sometimes it is even scary!!

I realize that these sections are short, but they are straight to the point. I don't believe in trying to fill a page up with words so it looks longer. I merely write what needs to be written and leave it at that. I am sure that any potential future volumes on this topic will increase in size and quality. I feel that writing down family stories is important, just as my ideals in this book. Stories tend to become lost or altered over time, so a written record is always in order.

This can also be the case in any area of family history as well as Indian blood stories. When the stories occurred long ago, the stories have to pass through more generations before it gets to you. By that time, it probably has changed a few times. The further back the original story, the more chance that you risk a change. That is where I am lucky in the case of my Cherokee ancestry. My great grandfather, passed it directly to my grandmother and my mother personally. In turn, they told it directly to me. There has been little time for stories to be lost or changed. In many families, their Indian blood may have occurred back in the 1600's.

I read somewhere that the average person with Indian heritage is only about 1/128 or less. That is a good ways from the beginning and stories can really be altered in time. This is another reason why I chose to write family books, as well as the one that you are reading now. As my family grows through the generations, I want as much information to be available as possible. No better way than to write it down and see that it gets passed on. You really have to think of the future when you do a family research, because it will benefit your descendants the most. Would not it have been great for you to have found a genealogy book that your great great grandfather had written long ago! Most of the time, this is not the case and the burden is on you. If you are doing the research, then you are the chosen one to pass the knowledge down to those after you.

More of My Views

With the above in mind, it is a good time to give you an idea of what comes next. As part of my views as a mixed blood Native American, I feel that honoring that heritage is of utmost importance. As we have discussed that some do not know or care about such a lineage, I believe that those that who do should take advantage of it. It is my belief that our ancestors would have wanted us to remember them. Although we hear how many hid the heritage and left the tribe to seek another life, the pride is still there. I have never viewed those families as ones who were ashamed of who they were. It was a matter of survival and the will to seek a better, safer life for their children. Without accusing them of selling out to white society, can you really blame them if you were in their shoes? We can form many opinions today, from the safety of our homes. We can even proclaim our Native American heritage without fear of being removed to Indian Territory. We can all vote and sit in the same seats on buses. Maybe with all of this freedom, it is easy for some people to tell you that your family could not have been Indian due to lack of records. Those same people would have probably hid their heritage also if they felt that they would have survived.

This is a real big problem in the world of genealogy today. When many people hear of Indian blood in their family, they begin the research process only to find nothing. Certainly, in some cases it may simply not exist. On the other hand, their family may fall into the category of mixed bloods or full bloods that we just discussed. Couple this with the family denying that heritage, and pretty soon you have a near impossible aspect of your lineage that can be proven on paper. As you will see, that is practically all that there is in the field of genealogy. According to most genealogists, paper trails make up your family history. I beg to differ on that ideal somewhat.

While paper trails are fine and needed in some cases, they are not everything. When you are dealing with a family that purposely hid their heritage, papers will mean very little to you in that respect. Their plan was to keep their heritage off of papers and from the eyes of their neighbors. This creates a genealogical nightmare that takes years to overcome. This is where I have argued with many researchers in the past. There are some by-the-book researchers that are so head strong that if they cannot find something on paper, then there is no possible way that it could have existed. Of course, there is some truth to that in some areas; however, that idea is not exclusive.

It appears that it is hard for some to believe that any Native American or mixed blood could have possibly hidden their heritage and assimilated into white society. No matter how hard I try, I still cannot grasp why that is so hard to believe. I will go deeper into this in a later chapter, but I feel that I must discuss it now also. It tends to anger me when people tell others that mention Indian blood in their family that there is not a smidgen of truth to it. Keep in mind that this normally comes from a third party who knows nothing of the individuals family at all. I find it hard to understand how someone else can tell me about my own family. Maybe our ancestors got tired of the government telling them similar things, such as whether their tribe could remain or disband. I realize that I am beginning to go off on a tangent here, but I feel that it still pertains to who I am, thus these thoughts are written as they come to mind.

Just as another personal example in reference to the hiding of Indian heritage, or I should say in reference to some that seldom speak of their heritage. As I have mentioned in this book, I have a neighbor whose grandmother grew up on the Cherokee Indian Reservation in North Carolina. I have known who this man was practically all of my life, as he is a well known person in my home town. Only until recently, did I even know that he was Cherokee. I don't think that he was hiding it, as much as the fact that he just didn't broadcast it to everyone. I know that he is not ashamed of his heritage, but merely doesn't go around with a sign on his head that states that he is Cherokee. This just goes to prove my point. There are people everywhere with Native American blood and they all do not live within the tribe's boundaries. Of course, there are some genealogists that would probably not believe that this gentleman was Cherokee unless he showed them his *papers*. How sad this society has become.

You will not want to put this book down until you have at least read the forthcoming chapter titled *The Story of Me*. I will go into greater discussion on topics that relate to what we are talking about now. I just can't seem to write enough on these subject areas though. I have gotten so aggravated with people in the past that insist on telling others about their own families. Is it too much to ask that one should believe that no one can tell you who you are better than your own people? This all stems back to the old days when the government wanted to wipe every bit of Indian blood from the face of the Earth. That sounds harsh, but it is more truthful than you know. The federal government wanted to place all of the Native Americans in Indian Territory, and it gave the appearance that they were at least trying to compensate them for the inconvenience. In reality, that was an inconvenience for the federal government themselves. They would have rather seen all of the Indians simply disappear than for them to have to give them any thing.

Have you ever heard of the Indian boarding schools that existed years ago? If you want a good example of what they were like, then I would recommend that you view a video titled *Lakota Woman*. In this film, they follow a young woman's struggle to find out who she is. It ends up at a siege at Wounded Knee, but I will not tell you what happens. You will have to see the film to find out! Anyway, as a young Lakota girl, she and her sister are sent to a Catholic boarding school out west. It shows them when they arrive at the school and this is where my point is made. They cut the girls braids out of their hair and make them wear uniforms. They pour powder on their heads, which is evidently a treatment for lice and continue to strip them of all of their native identity. From my opinion, it appears that they were being treated like animals. Such a sad picture. Schools like this did exist and many old ones alive today may have attended one of them.

Another film that I recommend to you is *The Education of Little Tree*. I think that this film is one of the greater stories about the Cherokee that I have seen portrayed on the silver screen. In this film, a young boy that is called Little Tree is raised by his white grandfather and his Cherokee grandmother. They live in the mountains of Tennessee. It shows how

Little Tree is raised with Cherokee values and taught many of the old ways by his grandparents. You really can see how peaceful their lives were living up there in that cabin in the mountains. Whenever they would go into town, you could see how people did not treat them well at all. The boy's grandfather makes moonshine by trade and teaches Little Tree to do the same. His grandmother home schools him, since she is the only one that can read and write.

Anyway, pretty soon some government agents come looking for Little Tree. A relative had filed a complaint against the grandfather for exposing the boy to an illegal trade. Anyhow, Little Tree is on the Cherokee rolls and is to be sent to an Indian school. Just as in Lakota Woman, when Little Tree arrives, he is given a new name, new clothes, and warned never to speak in his native tongue again. He and the other children are treated extremely bad throughout their stay at the school. I could go on, but I don't want to spoil this one for you either!

The moral of this film was that it showed how people wished to strip the Indian from the individual. When Little Tree was given a new name from a list that the school master had, it just showed how hiatus that people were. How demoralizing that must have been for people to be given a name that *someone else* thought was better! When he was warned not to speak in his native tongue, it was just another example of racial genocide. In essence, you can see that the goals of such a school was to take away their pride, heritage, and honor of who they truly were. I will never understand how our nation developed such ideals and tactics.

Between both of the above films, there is truth to all of them. They were not dramatized to entertain you. They were based on fact. You may find that hard to believe, but just ask some older ones that lived through times such as that about how it really was. I have had people tell me about how poorly their grandparents were treated by neighbors because they knew that they were mixed blood Indians. I have heard tales of people throwing rocks at them when they came out into their yards. It all sounds like something that I have made up to impress you, but it is not. It shouldn't impress you anyway, but should make you understand more why some chose to hide their heritage if they could. When you look at how the Indians were here first and the white man took their land, identity, and pride, it should also help you to understand whey some are adamant towards the government.

Maybe my last statement could be altered somewhat. Their land was taken, but maybe I should have said that the white man *attempted* to take their pride, identity, and honor. I doubt that any one or any entity could take that from America's first people. Even so, the scars still remain.

The sad part of this story is the fact that it should have been the other way around. The Indians should have been the ones who were having to decide whether to give the white man anything or not. Maybe the white man should have been the ones that had to adhere to the Indian way of life. After all, who was here first? Haven't we all grown up to hear the old saying, *finders are keepers*? It appears that the Native Americans were the first to be on North American soil. Shouldn't they have been the ones to decide whether the settlers were allowed to stay or leave? I was attending the Occaneechi-Saponi Homecoming Powwow this past May, and saw a shirt that was being sold by one of the vendors that caught my attention. I actually got a good laugh from it, because it spoke the truth. It read "*in 1492, the Indians discovered Columbus lost at sea!*" I doubt that any one statement could have said it better.

I know that we could go on and on concerning this subject. I also realize that this is a heavily discussed topic with the Native American circuit and rightly so. We also have to realize that it happened, and we will never be able to go back and change it. The damage has been done and that is just the way it is. You might even say that the influx of settlers and the destruction of the tribal lands was an inevitable change that was destined to occur. Whether it happened long ago or just yesterday, I feel that it would have come anyway. Do I hold a chip on my shoulder concerning what has happened? Yes and no. The positive side to that question is that if you are of Native blood, there almost has to be some resentment within you for the wrongs done to your ancestors. The negative answer to that question should be one of reason. Although it happened and you should be mindful of what your ancestors went through, you should move on.

If we go around with a bad attitude for what people did many years ago, we create a detrimental outlook on life from our on standpoint. The anger would continue to grow like cancer, eating away at what happiness that you can experience today. It is called picking up the pieces and moving forward. I see tribes doing that today and it is good. Granted, there are some that are in the mist of some pretty hard battles even to this day. Maybe those are justified in remaining harsh towards all that has happened. Many of the tribes out west are below poverty and you would be shocked at what they have to deal with. This is everywhere, but is worse in some places. Other than those that are having such a hard time, we should strive to grow as a proud people that will never die.

Look at it this way. If Native Americans stay angry and simply give up, they are basically telling the government that they won. You've got us. We are staying downtrodden as you wanted us to. On the other hand, if they can keep moving forward with survival in mind, the battle is never over. As humans, we all face battles each and every day. Some face more battles than others. Certainly it is no exception in the realm of Native America. I have heard some Indian people say how angry they are at Uncle Sam and how they would like to get back at them some how for the wrongs that were done. I completely understand the anger and would not try to convince them otherwise. However, I can make a suggestion as I have already discussed above. By moving on and becoming even a stronger, more sufficient people, you will be getting back at Uncle Sam. This shows that you are not what the old federal government told people that you were. And that was savage people that can not be civilized. Sounds pretty bad, but don't think that I just made that up. History proves it as fact.

I have said it over and over, but I cannot say it enough. The general population today have no idea of how bad it really was long ago for the Native Americans. The removal, discrimination, killings, slavery and out right inhuman treatment were all despicable crimes against our people in the old days. What few understand today is to what degree these things happened back then. It was much worse than any history book can describe. I cannot describe it in this book for the simple reason that I was not there, but also because there are some things that just cannot be put properly into words. Many of the elders of the tribes can tell you about how things were in their own life times. The discrimination has survived even to our days. Maybe it is not as bad today as it was years ago, or maybe it still is in some areas?

My own grandmother and aunts used to warn us about telling people that we had Cherokee blood in our veins. Granted, we lived about 15 minutes east of the City of Charlotte and not on a reservation. This did not matter to the rest of the world. As a matter of fact, this may have even made it worse. Because you did not live in an Indian settlement with others, you were own your on. That can be a lonely feeling if your neighbors harbor racist feelings towards you because some of your ancestors were not white. At one time, Native Americans were considered lower than African American slaves. I have read some accounts that stated that owning a slave was chattel property compared to an Indian. What were people thinking?

I know that I have said a mouthful thus far. I may have even deceived you in to thinking that this chapter did not contain such thoughts. It is still part of who I am. It is all related to me and my family. I may not have been there during the course of some of the events mentioned herein and I thank God that I didn't have to see them. It would just make it harder on me today. If I had lived through those things, I am sure that this book would be written in a completely different context. In any rate, this is just one more chapter in my story. My greatest goal for this chapter was to give you an idea of why many families hid their heritage, and why we must be proud of them today. This leads us to the next chapter, which deals exactly with that topic...*Honoring Your Ancestors.*

Chapter Five

Honoring Your Ancestors

I could not complete this book without this chapter. I have thrown so many thoughts at you already, and still the best is yet to come! However, this chapter is an important one nonetheless. Even though I explain many of the problems associated with researching and living the mixed blood life, the bottom line is to perpetually honor your ancestors for what they endured. We may feel that there is discrimination today and certainly it does still exist to a degree; however, our ancestors lived through much more than we will ever see in our life times. I hope that you understand that from the last chapter. It is that idea that should fuel your drive to honor your native ancestors. Whether mixed blood, full blood, enrolled or not, it should all be the same. When we begin to divide amongst ourselves, our people become weaker.

As I have mentioned and will say it again, this is not a book on how to be Indian. There is no such book available. This book cannot possibly begin to explain what it really means to be of Native American heritage. I cannot portray to you the problems associated with the same, nor can I put into the words the pride that I feel for such a heritage.

During this chapter, I will explore many different ways that I have honored my ancestors and if you choose, you may follow the same path. If not, just remember that each one's path is different. What I feel honors my ancestors, may not fill the bill with you. That is okay. Do what you feel is right in your heart. Just remember that they would want to be remembered.

The Powwow

The following section is an excerpt with revisions from one of my prior books, *Completing the Circle: The Hathcock Indian Blood*. I have added some things and have taken away some things. I felt that this section was most appropriate to include in this chapter. The reason being that I feel that you can gain a closer understanding of your ancestor's culture if you get involved today. This is especially true when one grows up as a mixed blood descendant of one of the tribes that had little exposure to the culture. You could say that learning more about your past later in life is better than not knowing at all. Visit the powwow and observe. You might be surprised what you can learn and who you might meet! Also keep in mind that many things that you may see at a powwow may be new culture. Some things are ages old and some are new. This demonstrates progress and advancement, as well as the ability to hold onto ancient culture.

The Native American powwow is probably one of the most well known ceremonies that our people hold. Powwows are for the most part a public affair that can last one day or more. They are normally held during the Spring and Summer months, but could occur at any time the tribe sees fit. Many people think that powwows are nothing more than a bunch of Indians getting together to get drunk and cause a scene. This is so far from the truth that it is silly! I could not think of a better place to take your family on a Saturday evening for some fun and cultural exposure. If you have never been to one, I highly recommend that you do and see for yourself.

Before I go any further on this topic, let me say that I do not claim to be an expert on this on any other topic in this book. I am simply a student in the game of life as we all are. If you find that something I explain appears different than how you personally observed it, then it may be. Some powwows may be a bit different than others anyway. The following is what I have perceived from being involved with them for the last few years. I enjoy attending them and have danced in the circle. It is a wonderful experience.

The powwow is only about 100 years old and began in Oklahoma. It has basically stemmed from traditions long ago when our ancestors danced around the fire in a circle for ceremonial reasons. Some of the dances have changed as well as other aspects, but the basic idea is still there. You will see old and new traditions being displayed at powwows. The powwow and heritage festival that I attended with the Occaneechi on May 8th 1999 was an outstanding event. It was like a family reunion for all of the Saponi people and we had great time. There was a large crowd who came to see all of the activities and it appeared that all had a good time.

What will you see at a powwow? This may vary from place to place, but they are all somewhat the same since they originated from one place. You will see dancing, both old and new, vendors selling crafts and food, exhibitions of Native American art and skills, as well as ceremonies that honor a particular person or tribe. It is very colorful and exciting! Normally, the grounds will open up early in the morning and all of the vendors will be hard at work selling their wares. At noon, or Indian time, the Grand Entry will take place. This is how the powwow works in our tribe, and probably the same in other localities. The dancing will go on all day and sometimes into the night. Most powwows are several days in length, but many will be only one or two days. At night, many will get together and have their own meetings and fun after the powwow is over. This is a time for family and friends to get together and sing songs or just talk about the days of old.

The Grand Entry is when the dancers first enter the arena or the Sacred Circle. Of course, there are some things that take place before this happens. The circle is blessed by a respected chosen elder who places tobacco around the circle as well as smudging herbs all around the arena. A prayer is prayed in English and in the tribes' language and then the dancers are ready to come in. There is also a certain order that dancers fall into while entering the circle for the Grand Entry. The veterans of the US armed forces are honored by allowing them to enter before the head man and lady dancers. The men's cloth and buckskin traditional dancers come in next. The women come in last and are arranged according to which type of regalia they are wearing such as buckskin dresses or fancy shawl regalia. There probably is some variance at other powwows, but this is how I have seen it done.

After the dancers enter the circle in a clockwise direction,(some tribes go the other way), the veterans song comes next. The veterans go to the center of the circle and the remaining dancers line the outer perimeter of the circle. The veterans song is played and all members of the audience will remove any headgear if wearing it. After the veterans song, and any other special song that the MC wishes to have sung, the powwow begins. The MC will call the songs and let you know if it is an intertribal or traditional song. There are also other dances that can occur such as the social dance (two step) or the crow hop. You will see fancy dancers and grass dancers. These often have the most elaborate regalia, although it is all such a sight to see. There can also be special dances that are considered sacred and cannot be photographed. The MC will normally tell you what can or cannot be photographed. It is not good etiquette to take pictures without permission and remember to *never* take any pictures when the circle is being blessed before the dancing begins.

If you wish to photograph a particular dancer, then ask his or her permission and then only take it after they have exited the circle. Maybe you could send them a copy of it when it comes back from the developers as a gesture of thanks. It is also customary to give a gift of tobacco when you need to thank someone or as an exchange for something. You will see many dancers with a tobacco pouch on their side maybe just for that purpose. Tobacco is considered a scared plant and it used in ceremonies. Contrary to our overindulgence of the sacred plant today, tobacco was not originally used as a habit.

If you wish to learn to dance then start going to powwows and watching the other dancers. You can also read some books and watch videos taken from other events. Normally, children were taken into the circle at a young age and danced with their parents so that they could imitate what they were doing. If you have to learn later in life, that's okay too. Just watch for few times and practice on you own at home. You cannot learn if you don't get out there and do it! Some powwows require that you meet certain criteria before you will be allowed to dance with them. Just make sure that you get permission from the hosting tribe or inquire whether you can dance with them or not. If not, respect the tribe's policies and enjoy simply being there!

Learning Your Native Tongue

I feel that there is nothing that can bring you closer to your heritage than to learn to speak the language of your ancestors. It may not seem that way to you, but that is how I look at it. You may never wish to attempt to do this and that is okay too. It would take some time and study to accomplish this task, but you can do it if you try. I spend some time studying the Cherokee language. I am not a fluent speaker as of yet, but I hope to get there one day. This has really opened my eyes even further to the way it used to be. One of the books that I have is narrated on tape by Sam Hider and co-authored by Gregg Howard. It is titled *Introduction to Cherokee*. This has been one of the easiest books to use as it came with some cassette tapes to help you pronounce the words. Although not a complete language course, it can give you a great deal of vocabulary. In this book, it states that learning the Cherokee language will create a change in your life. I think that they were right.

As you can see, I still am using the Cherokee or Tsalagi as an example. It doesn't matter which tribe that you descend from, it is still the same principle. If you are Lakota, then study that language. If you are Choctaw, then do the same. Unless you descend from one of the smaller tribes that disbanded in the early 1700's, you should be able to locate some good resources for language study. Although, many of the smaller tribes merged with larger nations and adopted their language. For example, the Occaneechi merged with several other tribes at Fort Christanna in the 1700's, thereby they spoke Tutelo-Saponi. Even that language is being revived by the tribe with the help of the University of North Carolina at Chapel Hill. Just do some research, I am sure that you can find what you are looking for.

Do Some Reading

In addition to the study of your native language, you might want to do some studying on the history of your tribe. If you are involved in family research, you cannot avoid this. This is especially true when you are unsure of the tribe that you descend from. See the section in this book that deals with research tips. You will find more on that topic there. Anyway, if you know your tribe and wish to learn more, then nothing will help you more than spending some time reading up on their history. I know that in dealing with the Cherokee, there are numerous books out there that give an accurate account of the tribe's history. Some other tribes may be a bit more difficult to research, but you should be able to find something out there.

I think that this honors your ancestors for the reason that you are interested in them. You want to know more about them, which in turn teaches one who you are. I find that it will draw you much closer to your heritage if you can know about what the old days were like. Just like in the last chapter, where I told you about how bad the early days were. You will find many events recorded in books that maybe you did not know about. It is always better to know than not. It will also give you the ability to relate to your tribe better today. If you are applying for tribal membership, but cannot have an intelligent conversation with the tribe concerning who they are, they are going to view your interest differently. I realize that if you meet certain requirements, then you are entitled to enroll, but that is not the point.

You can carry one hundred membership cards, but still know nothing of who your people are. It is my belief that if you are going to go all the way with your heritage, then do so. I would actually feel kind of foolish showing someone my enrollment card, but yet could not tell them anything about the trail of tears and why I carry the card in the first place! It is not a requirement to take a history test to join any tribe, that I know of. However, doesn't it say something about you as a Native American? Doesn't it show that you are coming back to your people because you desire to be reunited and not for some type of gain? Since there is a great deal of that today, as well as years ago, I would rather for people to know how I really stood.

Of course, you may not choose to do this either and that is fine. I just think that if you truly care about your past, then you would want to know more. I realize that many people do not like to read or study. I am completely guilty of that due to the fact that high school was a drag to me! Sounds crazy coming from an author, but it is the truth. On the other hand, if you are reading this book, then you have already shown me that you possess a genuine interest in learning more. At least get a basic background of the people that you come from. When you do this, I assure you that it will be a rewarding journey that will enrich many aspects of your life.

Talk to People

If you have the luxury of knowing some tribal elders, then you have a wealth of knowledge at your fingertips. I doubt that you could learn from a book what some of the old people could tell you. They have been around longer than you and have seen much more take place. Many of them would love to be able to tell you some stories. Just like my grandfather, it just lights up their eyes when you are interested enough to ask them questions. Many of them have stories locked in their hearts that are just dying to be revived. On the other hand, you may meet some that simply wish to be left alone. You have to respect them no matter which way they choose to be. I am not telling you to show up on the reservation and expect an elder to take you in and train you in the medicine. I am just saying use common sense and be polite to those that you do know or meet. It is easier to get someone to talk to you if they know and trust you.

My girlfriend's father told me that I should talk to the elders. He said that is where the knowledge is. He was raised by his full blood grandmother in the mountains of North Carolina. I agree with him and that is why I am telling you. Besides elders of the tribe, talk to your own family members. This subject is also covered in my research tips chapter, but it has relevance here also. In this respect, some of your family may be glad to tell you what they know about their past. It is important to remember that you may run up on some family members that do not wish to talk about their heritage. Just explain to them why you want to know and maybe that will make them change their minds. If the choose not to tell you, then you will just have to honor their request and realize that they probably have a good reason for wanting to keep it quiet. Maybe it all falls back onto what we discussed earlier. That should help you to understand better.

These are only a few methods of honoring your ancestral ties. I have some more information that I wish to share with you, but felt that I needed to place it in a chapter of it's own. This next chapter still involves what you can do to honor your ancestors by tracing your family tree. I have included some pointers that may help you in your search. Here again, this is not written in stone and by no means do I say that these are the only ways to accomplish this task. In the same respect, these are not the only ways that you may choose to honor your ancestors. With this in mind, let's proceed on to some pointers that may help you find your roots. Remember that I said that this is not a genealogy book and it is not. I do not have any records included here or necessarily any particular books listed to go read. I just wanted to incorporate the idea that seeking your roots is a way to keep your heritage alive for generations to come!

Maybe you don't feel that by researching your family you are honoring your ancestors. Look at it this way. If you had suffered discrimination and other tribulations during your life time, wouldn't you want your future generations to remember you for what you went through? Think of how proud they were of who they were and how they loved their homelands. Ponder how the white man attempted to strip every bit of this from them. Maybe many did lose their land, freedom, and other possessions; however, no one could touch what was in their hearts. Remember that many hid their heritage in order to escape ill treatment towards themselves and their children. Especially, remember the trail where they cried. With these ideas at the forefront of our minds, how could we think that honoring our ancestors by any means possible is a futile effort? I hope that by now you can clearly see my points. So maybe something as simple as filling in those blank spots in your family history and learning of their culture is much more important than one would think.

The next chapter was one that I felt was a bit difficult to find the right place for, but after some thought I decided that it should come immediately after this chapter. It falls into the category of honoring my ancestors, but deserved a place of it's own. After you read through it, you will be ready to proceed on with *Researching Your Native Past*. I warned you that my style of writing is different. When thoughts come to mind, I have to place them where I feel that they should be. Although it may seem that this book is collection of many subjects, it all fits together nicely once you digest it in it's entirety. In some respects, you could pick this book up and begin at any section and still get a great deal of meaning from it. However, I would prefer that you start at the beginning and continue on till the end. Just stay with me, it will all come together! When you are ready, proceed on to the next chapter.

Chapter Six

The Land of 1000 Smokes

As I told you at the close of the last chapter, this one was hard to place in a proper location. At first, it was part of the proceeding chapter. After some thought, I felt that this would have to be in a place of it's own, as I explained already. Sometimes ideas can be blended in with others, but I feel that it takes away from the importance of them a bit. This chapter has a very deep meaning to me, as you will see. You might say that it is a family thing! One important aspect to note before you read this. Get ready for some very deep thought. This is probably the most artistic chapter in this book. Prepare for an experience! If you read each word and pay attention to what you are reading, I will paint the most vivid scene in your mind's eye. You may even smell the mountain air.

The title of this chapter is one that should draw your interest or curiosity. Maybe some of you have heard this mentioned before. If not, then I will go ahead and tell you that the Land of 1000 smokes refers to the Great Smoky Mountains. Many of the Cherokee will know them as the title of the chapter has described. You might could guess how they got that name. If you visit the Great Smoky Mountains, particularly on a cool day, it will look as if each mountain is a smoke stack giving off the whitest steam. I can think of no other beautiful scene that God could have created.

I spend a great deal of time at the Cherokee Indian Reservation located in the Great Smoky Mountains of North Carolina. I currently live about three hours east of them and hope to be moving there in the future. At one time, I was discussing with my mother about moving elsewhere in order to be better motivated to write. Since writing has become such an important passion for me, I look at it as a grand investment not to be taken lightly. I told her that I really love North Myrtle Beach, South Carolina and I spend some time there also. The Ocean Drive area is my utmost favorite. When discussing this with her, she told me that I would be much better off in the Smokies. I think that her reasoning goes much deeper than just the fact that it is a more beautiful place to be.

In several places of this book, you have seen me make reference to my maternal great grandfather Lambert, from whom my Cherokee lineage was passed down from. He also spent a great deal of time in Cherokee, NC and took the family with him on several occasions. It was during those times that he reminded the family that we had relatives there. The other day, I drove passed Mary Lambert Farm Road on the reservation, and I was reminded of my great grandfather. You know how it is. You can see a name and it just sparks thoughts that begin to flow in your head. Grandpa Lambert loved the Smokies and I can only guess why. It pleases my mother to see me carry on so many things that she had watched her grandfather do. Her father died when she was a young lady and her grandfather became one of utmost importance to her. That is what I meant above when I said that it was a *family thing*.

Since I told you that this chapter was directly related to honoring my ancestors, I will clarify that even deeper. Besides carrying on a love that my great grandfather had for this area, it is also a very special place to the Cherokee. The Cherokee can be called the original inhabitants of the Smokies and I can understand why they chose to stay in such a place. The beauty is indescribable, the atmosphere is most peaceful, and my ancestral ties to them make the circle complete. That is a mouthful! If you are Cherokee, I am sure that you can grasp what I am getting at.

As I wonder from the flat lands back to the mountains, a sense of excitement always overcomes me. I can only describe it as a small child preparing to open a gift on Christmas morning. What will I get today? What beauty will God reveal to me on this journey into the mountains? What glimpse of majestic scenery will the Great Smoky Mountains grant me this time? All of these questions build to an ultimate climax when I step from my car and take that first breath of clean mountain air.

Whenever I first arrive in Cherokee, my first item of business is to take a long look across the hazy skyline. The lazy ridge meets the sky in perfect form, as if they were just meant to be admired by everyone that would dare to take a glimpse at it's beauty. As I stand there looking across the mountains, I am reminded of the old days when the Cherokee were being forced to leave such a natural wonder. Not only was it such a beautiful place to admire, it was home. This had been their home for such a long time, how could one expect them to go peacefully unto a strange land?

I often wonder what my ancestors thought as they gazed across the smoky ridges in their ancestral homelands. Surely they wondered how something as mighty as these hills could have been created. There is no way to gaze upon this natural phenomena and say that there is no God. Only a foolish man could utter such a blasphemous remark. Another thought comes to mind when taking that same look. The mountains show no prejudice and are the same everyday. The rich and the poor can gaze upon their presence without debt. When the snow falls, it does so on everyone. It creates a beautiful blanket on everything that it touches. Shouldn't we be the same way? Shouldn't we respect everyone? Isn't it amazing that you could learn something so valuable from an inanimate object?

There also comes an air of mystery when one looks upon the enormous sleeping giants. They seem to be keeping secrets from us that can only be revealed if we should seek them. It is no wonder that the Cherokee had so many legends that were inspired by this majestic land. To be so quiet, but yet they could tell us so many stories should God allow them to cry out. If we could only be there to listen if they would.

On many cool mornings, I awoke to see a deep blanket of fog covering the mountains. It would come right down and kiss you on the cheek as you stepped outside to greet the morning. The moist air would feel as if it was going right through you when you took a deep, relaxing breath.

Besides the beauty and the cool morning mist, the sounds of silence deafen your ears. In this modern day world with super highways, sirens, and exhaust fumes, one can only hope to obtain relief from such an experience. Many do not like silence. Maybe it is because we are just too busy to listen to it's calming presence. Someone once told me that in order to learn, you have to listen, and it order to listen you have to be quiet. The answers to many of our questions are only a whisper away, but yet we neglect so great an opportunity to hear them. I find a restful peace in hearing the mountains speak in silence.

During another one of my stays on the reservation, I went for a jog along a road that runs parallel to the Oconaluftee River. Being an avid runner when my arthritis is not causing me grief, I find it a fairly easy exercise. Without worrying about how hard it is, I can spend more time enjoying what I pass as I run down the road. That day, the river was rushing swiftly and I could hear it bubbling across the smooth river stones. I could almost smell the water as the breeze rushed through the river. It seemed to give me a boost of energy and took my mind off of the pain that any run will give you. I found myself drifting away in thought as I watched the river go past me each time I struck the ground.

The river is also a gift from the Creator. The Oconaluftee appears to come straight from the Smokies as if they were leaving a trail for you to follow up and into it's arms. The waters beckon you to taste it's coolness and feel the healing power that the Cherokee discovered long ago. Another wonder of nature that is neglected by so many.

I have often heard people say that nothing is free in this world. However, I beg to differ with that statement. There are plenty of blessings in this world that are free for the asking. The problem is that we do not ask, nor do we seek their gifts. I feel that the emotions that flood my soul as I look upon the Great Smoky Mountains are one of those gifts. The beauty of those mountains and the rivers that run about them like a snake that encircles it's prey, are also part of those gifts. Will you be willing to receive them with open arms? They are there just waiting to be discovered.

God has granted us the temporary enjoyment of each of these gifts that I have described. Just as the Cherokee have done so for many years, I too plan to accept each and every experience that they can give. What may seem like just a day in the mountains to others, was a journey into the Land of 1000 Smokes for me.

Chapter Seven

Researching Your Native Past

I have mentioned it many times and here it is. These are some tips that you may find useful as a researcher seeking your family roots. Many of you may be experienced researchers and others may not be. In any rate, I have included this section to help get you started if you choose to investigate your heritage yourself. As a matter of fact, I recommend it! Whether you choose to do a standard research project, or an Indian heritage search, I think that it is good to spend time on such a thing. It will be a challenge, but the results of your efforts will be worth it. I am not claiming to be an expert on the subject, but have just spent many hours doing it. You can really learn by getting out there and doing the work! This is another one of those sections that have extracted from my earlier writings. Sometimes I feel that this book is like a puzzle that had been scattered across the living room floor. I finally found all of the pieces and put it together to make a proper picture!

Below is a report that I felt would be beneficial to include in this section in regards to obtaining vital records. You will hear that term quite a bit once you begin researching. Vital records include birth, death, and marriage certificates that ultimately become housed at the State level. Of course, older marriage documents that were created before the 1900's will probably only be housed at the County level. This report below was included in an informational package that I purchased the reprint rights to. It does contain some useful information, but I will cover vital records myself later.

Guide to Obtaining Vital Records

As part of its mission to provide access to data and information relating to the health of the Nation, the National Center for Health Statistics produces a number of publications containing reference and statistical materials. The purpose of this publication is solely to provide information about individual vital records maintained only on file in State or local vital statistics' offices. An official certificate of every birth, death, marriage, and divorce should be on file in the locality where the event occurred. The Federal Government does not maintain files or indexes of these records. These records are filed permanently either in a State vital statistics office or in a city, county, or other local office.

To obtain a certified copy of any of the certificates, write or go to the vital statistics office in the State or area where the event occurred. Addresses and fees are given for each event in the State or area concerned. To ensure that you receive an accurate record for your request and that your request is filled expeditiously, please follow the steps outlined below for the information in which you are interested.

Write to the appropriate office to have your request filled. Under the appropriate office, information has been included for birth and death records concerning whether the State will accept checks or money orders and to whom they should be made payable. This same information would apply when marriage and divorce records are available from the State office. However, it is impossible for us to list fees and addresses for all county offices where marriage and divorce records may be obtained.

For all certified copies requested, make check or money order payable for the correct amount for the number of copies you want to obtain. Cash is not recommended because the office cannot refund cash lost in transit. Because all fees are subject to change, a telephone number has been included in the information for each State for use in verifying the current fee.

Type or print all names and addresses in the letter. Give the following facts when writing for birth or death records: Full name of person whose record is being requested, Sex, Parents' names, including maiden name of mother, Month, day, and year of birth or death, and Place of birth or death (city or town, county, and State; and name of hospital, if known). Also include the purpose for which copy is needed, and the relationship to person whose record is being requested.

For marriage records, give the following facts: Full names of bride and groom, month, day, and year of marriage, place of marriage (city or town, county, and State), purpose for which copy is needed, and the relationship to persons whose record is being requested.

When writing for divorce records, give the following facts when writing for divorce records: full names of husband and wife, date of divorce or annulment, place of divorce or annulment, type of final decree, purpose for which copy is needed, and the relationship to persons whose record is being requested. Keep in mind that the above information is normally used when you have to contact the office by mail. If you go to the office in person, you can normally do the searching yourself. You will still need names and dates to aid you in your search.

As I stated above, when you go to find vital records, you will need to be aware that the State level does not house every record. Most older records will be located in the County that you seek, unless destroyed by a fire, etc. The County Register of Deeds Office should have records that date back to the date that the county was formed. Most of these older records include marriage certificates and land records. You probably will not find birth or death records back past the 1900's.

How can marriage certificates help you? First of all, it gives you a marriage date and location. Next, it should give you both parents names on each side and where they were from. Sometimes, when one or both parents are dead, the place they were from will be left blank as I found out on many of my records. This information can sometimes be the key to a sticking point that you have come to in your research. Do not neglect any type of old record! Some of the most trivial information that you find will lead you down a path to answers that you seek.

Before I go any further, let me just give you an idea of what you should try to collect once you know who you are looking for. First of all, the marriage and death certificates as we talked about above. Next, you will want to seek land records, obituaries, court records, census records, tax lists, and any other researcher's book that you can find on the family you seek. If you keep the above list in mind, you should have a wealth of information available to you once you know the correct names to look for.

Basic Research Principles

That brings us to the "meat" of the subject, looking for your relatives names. This is where the real research comes into play. It depends on how much knowledge you have up front that determines what course to take next. You will obviously want to start with family members who are still living, preferably your older relatives. They have stories and information that is locked in their heads just waiting to come out. Many of your older relatives love to talk about their families and appreciate your interest in your past. Take time to talk to them before they are gone. Once they pass away, the stories go with them!

You should then talk to any and all of your relatives. They might remember a story told to them by their grandmother or grandfather who has already passed on. Surprisingly, many people fail to find much information because they did not ask! Some of your family may have the key information, but don't ever think to tell you because they did not know you were searching for it. Make sure you interview every member of the family in that line. Once you do this, you will be surprised how many more names that you have in your files that you did not before you talked to them. Here again, remember what I told you earlier about being careful how you ask older relatives about their past. Whether it regards Indian heritage or simply something that they may not wish to talk about, just be reasonable and don't hound them about it. One example may be the tragic death of a loved one or simply something that they are trying to forget.

You should now have at least some great grandparents names to go with. This is usually enough to get you started even though it is not really that much information. When I started my research project on my mother's line, I only knew my great grand father's name and that was it. Today, I have over 2500 people listed in my family file! Of course, that is after two years of research. Once you have some older names, you will find that the marriage certificates will come in handy. Take your great grandparents names and located their marriage or death certificates. This will then give you your great great grandparents names. You should then be able to use the vital records that are housed in the appropriate county to do the same thing for one more generation back. Now you have your 3rd great grandparents names if all goes well.

Now, here is where it starts to get a bit more difficult. It is usually fairly easy to get back to about the Civil War era as long as you have the right names and places, but going further back starts the real challenge. Records ten to get scarce once you get past the 1860's. It is here that you will have to switch from using standard vital records to what I call *round about* record searching. This type of searching involves the type of other records that I mentioned earlier, such as tax lists, census lists, and land records. You will find that this is a bit more difficult and you really have to pay attention to what you are doing or you will get on the wrong path.

Another problem that you will run into here is that you will find that your relatives may not have lived where you thought they did. You may have thought that your family has lived in a certain county for many years, only to find out that they disappear off of the records past the 1900's! This could not be right! Oh yes it could. People moved around much more than you think in the 1800's. They moved to where the jobs and resources were. One line of my family lived all across Virginia and the Carolinas before settling in Cabarrus County, NC. Before I began my project, I thought that they had been here much longer than they were. In fact, one line of my family has lived in this county for less than 100 years and the others less that 60 years! Just don't assume anything.

You may find that your family moved more than you thought and the only way to track them is by census lists, tax lists, and land records. Keep in mind that the census was only taken every ten years. On the census indexes or the actual handwritten census pages, the head of the household will be listed. Depending on whether you are dealing with the 1850 or later census, most will only have codes and numbers in reference to the remaining members of the household. The later the census year, the more information that you will have access to. The 1900 census marked a new era for genealogists. It gave the most information that any census year had ever given. While not all of it necessarily would be of benefit for actual family tree purposes, it did give you much information about your ancestor.

I recommend that you start with the known, and work your way back to the unknown. In other words, if you only know who your great grandparents were, then you will need to start with them. The census is a wonderful tool and without it, I am not sure how difficult it would be to complete your research project. You can view the census in one of several ways. First of all, a company by the name of Heritage Quest has been a life saver. They scan census records onto CD-ROM that they call digital microfilm. This concept is wonderful for the genealogist that does not have the time to travel to repositories. For example, if you needed to view the 1870 census for Cabarrus County, North Carolina, you would simply order it from Heritage Quest by roll number requesting the digital microfilm version. You can also get the actual microfilm by purchasing it from them or by joining the organizations and renting it for 30 days at less than $4.00 per roll.

I realize that this is not a commercial for Heritage Quest, but I am a regular customer of theirs. The beauty of their CD-ROM idea is the fact that you do not need a microfilm viewer to look at the census schedules.

You can even zoom in on certain portions of the page with amazing clarity, and print it off the screen. As of this writing, the cost for each CD-ROM is around $15.00. This normally contains up to about three counties records on each disk. If you wanted the whole census for a particular state, it might be cheaper to rent the rolls themselves. Otherwise, this can be very convenient for you.

You can also purchase books that people have written which basically is a transcription of the census. I admire the authors of these books for taking the time to not only write out that much information, but also to decipher the handwriting that fills the census page. In case you do not know, old handwriting is somewhat different than today. You will even find abbreviations that you are not familiar with. It is amazing how even our forms of English have changed over the years. You will find terms and other notations that you may not understand. Also, often times the way that certain letters were formed are completely unfamiliar to you and it may be hard to read. Many of the census takers evidently weren't very educated and their writing skills were less to be desired.

You may also choose to visit your state archives, the national archives division, or even your local library. Each of these will normally house the census schedules for the local area plus others depending on which repository that you choose to visit. If this is the route that you plan to take, be prepared to wait on microfilm machines if it is crowded. You may be surprised to see how many people are doing the exact same thing that you are doing. Genealogy is a big business!

If you choose to go to a library or other repository to view the census records, then get you some blank census log forms and write every thing down about your particular family when you find them. This will keep you from having to go back and located the same record every time you need information. If researching in a library, ask them if you can photocopy the census page for personal use. They will usually allow you to do so. Census searching can be tedious and boring, but just hang on, you will find them if they are there.

Now keep in mind that I am speaking of general genealogy at this point. Indian research will begin just like this, but will take some sharp turns to the left at certain points. I will go into that later, but if you are searching for Indian relatives, then don't rely one hundred percent on census lists. They may not tell you what you are looking for. I will talk about Indian census lists and what to look for later on, but for now we will continue with regular research tactics.

I would use the federal census index for your state first. Why should you do this? First of all, if you do not know the county that you relatives lived in, then this will give you a broader search criteria. You will be able to search a larger geographical area with one source. Once you figure out which county, then you can go to the actual census page and locate the same relative there. When you get to the proper county, then more information will be waiting on you such as children's , husband's, or wife's name. Most will give the occupation of the head of household and how much land they owned. Each census year is a bit different with the amount of information that it gives you.

I have to stop and tell you one point about census lists. Keep in mind that they are not error free!! Some of the enumerators did not do a good job of recording information. You will find errors in spelling, ages, and other personal bits of information that you know to be an error. Now, make sure that it is an error. You may be wrong yourself! Cross check each suspected error with other documents to see if they match, then make the determination. You should keep an open mind when doing research anyway. Many times we find out that what our family told us was not correct. You may find that a certain person did not marry who you thought they did according to your family member. One personal example was when a relative of mine told me who my great grandfather's first wife was. I took it as face value and continued my research. The error was found on an old marriage certificate and the census records. The lady that was supposed to have been his first wife turned out to be his sister! It was not intentional, just a natural mix up that can occur when dealing with older ancestors.

I find it best not to try to argue with relatives nor correct them on the spot. Let them go ahead and tell you what they want to since they may not really know themselves. Do your own research and then present it to them without pointing a finger at them as being the one who was wrong. You can really upset your relatives if you tell them that something they said was "impossible" or "there's now way that could have been". Instead, present the evidence in a tactful manner, explaining to them what you found and then show them! Show them the actual documents and let them know that it is not uncommon for stories to change over the course of many years. This way, you will avoid hurting someone's feelings and that is not the purpose of researching your family tree. Can this occur in regards to Indian research? It most certainly can. You may have to be extra careful when dealing with that subject.

Once you have become satisfied with the results of your census searching, you may want to go on to tax lists from the colonial era. If you go back further than 1790, then that is all that you will have besides court and land records. The first federal census was taken in 1790 and then every ten years thereafter. You should be able to look at census lists up until about 1920. Every list from that year forward is still considered private information and has not been released to the public.

Here is a good time to include a point about private information. Whether you are writing a book about your family or posting it to the Internet, you should respect other's privacy. As a matter of fact, it is a legal issue. If your work is going to be made public, such as this book, then you will need to "clean" your family tree somewhat. What I mean by cleaning is to remove certain bits of information that can create problems for an individual if released. For example, do not include dates of birth on living individuals. Giving the year may be okay, but do not pin point all of the information. Giving out social security numbers, addresses, phone numbers, and other personal data is a big *no no*! People can use that information to obtain false credit accounts and other illegal ventures, so don't do it. Besides, that falls under laws governing privacy. Most records are public and are at your disposal, just use common sense and don't print anything that you would not print about yourself.

The next subject that I want to cover is organization of your work. This is probably one of the most important steps in research. If you do not keep your work organized, then you can really undo much of your work. If you lose what you worked so hard to find, then it is back to square one again! What I did was purchase one of those plastic file holders with a lid on it. Then, I took some folders and labeled each one with every family line that I was researching. I also labeled some "census", "general notes", "references", "Indian notes." This will help keep all of the papers in an organized manner. You will see what I am talking about once you get started. You will have papers and notes everywhere!!

Here is where we need to talk about note keeping. This is of an utmost importance! Every time that you acquire something new, be it census data, family statements, or whatever, write it down! The file folder will now come in handy. You have to keep in organized once you do write it down or it will still be of little value to you. I don't know how many times that I made that mistake before I learned to use the file system. Trust me on this one! You should write down everything that you find, no matter how trivial it may seem. You may find out that one piece of information that you did not write down was exactly what you were looking for. This happened to me and I had a real hard time going back and relocating the source again.

When interviewing family members, you may want to have them write their stories out for you. This way, you will know exactly what was on their minds. If not, then take good notes and do not leave out details and think that you will remember them later. Most of the time, you are working on more than one line at a time and the information can get crossed. As stated earlier, do not correct family members while you are interviewing them. If you feel that they are wrong, then you may want to ask some questions to find out where they got this information. As a matter of fact, you should always ask where they learned the story. They may have been told the family story from another person who is still living and that person should be next on your interview list.

You remember when I talked about *round about* record searching? That technique applies to family interviews also. You should always go off of your direct line to obtain information as well as to cross reference information that you already have. In other words, if you wanted information about your great grand father, then just don't stick to his direct lineal descent relatives. Talk to cousins, aunts and great aunts about him. Someone will have something to contribute that the others do not. I actually learned more about my great grandfather Lambert by talking to a cousin of mine than I did from others. The reason was the he lived with them most of his elderly life. My mother had information and my cousin had information. When I combined the two, I had a good background on grandpa Lambert. Make sure you try this technique so that you can close some loose ends in your search.

Now, I have covered a very basic approach to genealogy. This is not the only ways to do a search and do not limit yourself to what I have told you. I did not go into much detail, but this will get you on a very good track to finding out where you came from. You will find many dead ends and many people that just don't seem to fit where you thought they did. Do not give up! The evidence is there somewhere, you just have to find it. Be very flexible in your thinking as not every piece of information will turn out the way you thought it would. Make sure that you prove the relationships the best that you can. As in the case of my great grandfather's wife, I had to verify it myself. Had I not done so, then my great grandmother would have been in the wrong location on the family tree. One mistake way back in your family tree will throw your whole line off as it comes back to you.

Researching Your Tribe

This leads us into the main reason for this section, Indian research. As I stated before, I am not a certified Indian genealogist and don't claim to be. I went to Indian research school at the school of hard knocks! Everything that I have learned from this point on was from merely making mistakes and following the footsteps of other researchers. Indian research is hard work and in no other place are you going to find the *round about* research philosophy more useful. To track down Indian blood, you sometimes will feel as if you are looking for a needle in a haystack, as someone once said. Indian connections are not always as easy to see as you think. If you think that you have met some dead ends in your search so far, hold on because it gets harder!

Finding your Indian connection comes in steps. First of all, you have to have a reason to be looking for it. You may have heard family members talk about someone being *part Indian*. You may find that your last names are associated with an Indian nation that you have just grown up knowing about. In any rate, the search can all be similar. After hearing the stories, it is time to verify it. This is where the real work comes into play. The only time that this may not be as difficult is when you are connected to the Cherokee Nation and have a definite ancestor that was enrolled. The Cherokee seem to have some of the best kept census records that I know of. Starting in about 1817 until the present, the Cherokee have been enumerated by census takers for various reasons. Many were for land allotments and others were simply for the sake of knowing how many Cherokee were in the area. This wasn't always for the benefit of the tribe I can tell you.

If one of your ancestors was enumerated on one or more of the Cherokee rolls, then you are in luck. You will have a wealth of information at your fingertips. If they were not listed on the rolls, but you have been told you were Cherokee, then stand by, you will fall under the next step of research. The rolls are in print and offer the English as well as the

Indian name of the person in some cases. The Indian census of 1900 offers the tribal connection if you wish to check that one. In any rate, your Cherokee connection may be easier to find if you can relate to one of the rolls. If they don't, it is not an easy task if not an impossible one to prove. Just remember that how much proof you need is determined by what your goals are concerning your Native American heritage.

If you have been told of a specific tribe, then that is obviously where you should begin. That may end up being the wrong place, but at least you have a starting point. Many people, such as in my Hathcock line, did not know what tribe, only that they were Indian. This occurred in many families here in NC and VA. I have talked to many Indian people who simply did not know or care where there family belonged in the tribal history. This is a shame, but it happens. You are lucky if your family knew the tribe, so start there.

If you do know the tribe, then you should check that tribes current status to see if they are still active and have a tribal office. You may wish to write or call them and ask about your connection. They do not always respond and most do not have the time to help you research. Also, do not contact them until you have really done your homework. It is considered rude to ask someone to help you with your own research when you have not done any of the work yourself. So, make sure that you have plenty of ancestral names and information leading you to the tribe before contacting them. If they help you, that is great, but do not expect much. They are not obligated to establish your connection to their tribe and they have their own policies about giving out information. Many tribes keep their history and roll books closed to the public and there is nothing you can do about it. A friendly letter is not wrong though and maybe it will yield some results for you. If not, then the burden of research is still one hundred percent on you. You should always assume that it is anyway, that way if the tribe cannot offer you any information, then all will not be lost. I experienced that some when searching my Cherokee heritage.

If Your Tribe is Unknown

If you do not know the tribe or if the tribe does not offer you any information, then you will research the same way. This involves starting with nothing and locating something! This is difficult because you may find that you came from a tribe that was relatively small and maybe disbanded a long time ago. In any rate, the search is tough, but you can do it. The first thing that you need to do is get out all of you family notes and lay a map out on the table. By now, you should know exactly where your family was from and where all they moved to. If you have skipped the general genealogy part of this search, stop and go back!! You should not be at this point yet if you are still wondering such things as who your great grandparents were and where they lived. Your search for your Indian connection will be literally impossible if you are still asking such questions.

Assuming that you are ready, mark a dot on the map for every place that your family lived, whether it be in one or more states. Then make a note which family name is associated with that location. In other words, if you are researching your Hathcock line, then mark Hathcock at each dot. If the name had a variation in the spelling, then write that spelling at the appropriate place and list the date. It is important to put the dates beside of the dots on the map. This way you will be able to arrange your ideas and migratory patterns in a chronological manner. This is of utmost importance as you will see later.

Once you have that completed, it is time to go hit the books again. If you know the tribe or your family has given you a tribe's name, then you will want to go and find some history on that tribe. If you do not know the tribe, then check out some general Indian history books that are pertinent to the region that you family lived in. For example, if your family mainly came from the coast of NC, then you will want to check out which tribes lived in that area during the life time of your ancestors. In this case, it may be the Tuscorora. You should get the picture now. If you know the tribe, then go right to the history of that tribe. There are many books available about particular Indian tribes that may be of help.

If you cannot find the tribe that your family told you about, then you should try to find out if it was part of a larger nation. This was almost always the case when dealing with smaller tribal groups. One example would be my lineage. The Occaneechi were a distinct tribe, but were actually part of a larger nation, the Saponi. Most of the smaller tribes in the Piedmont of NC were Southeastern Sioux and fell under the Catawba Confederacy. The Catawba Confederacy was actually made up of about 24 smaller tribes or bands, the Occaneechi being one of them. As you can see, it is more difficult to trace than you think! Once you figure out if the tribe merged with a larger group, then you can search that larger nation for more details. It is there that you may find more about your family.

If you still do not know exactly what tribe and you were only told that you were Indian, then you have to take it back one more step. Here is where the map with your family locations cited on it really comes in handy. You should located the tribes in that area, as stated earlier. Then see which nations those tribes merged with. From that point, trace the migratory patterns of the tribes and note them on your map. You should make a different symbol for each one that you are tracking so as not to get confused. Once you feel that you have done a good job tracking the tribal movements, compare these movements to that of your family. Which ever one fits the closest may be your tribe. This is not always the case, but you can bet that it is fairly accurate if your family stayed with the tribe for any length of time.

If you find that you family does not follow the exact pattern of a particular tribe, then find the one that is closest. Go back on your timeline to the place where your family did live in the same area as one of the tribes. Then, research that tribe to see if you family was part of it, but just left the area. In my line of Hathcocks, this is what happened. We can trace their movements with the tribe for some time, then they branch off to the south. This may have happened to your family. Remember, many families left the tribal area in order to survive and have a better chance at living in a white world. This is not "giving up" on their people as some have said to me, but yet a means to survive and give their children a chance to live. No matter where the family went, your blood does not change. You are who you are no matter where your family resided.

Once you locate your family, though whatever means possible, it is then time to begin looking at the government rolls that were taken of some tribes. We will use the Cherokee as an example for such a venture. This usually where people run into the most problems associated with their search for Indian ancestors. The rolls were not really for the benefit of the Indians, although it appeared that they were in some cases. In any rate, we will take a look at one of the greatest problems in this area and that is the fact that you may not see your ancestor listed on the rolls.

Failing to Find Ancestors on the Rolls

One thought on the rolls before we move on. Although some will argue with me on this, not all people of Cherokee heritage are listed on the rolls. I have met countless genealogists who will tell you bluntly that if your ancestors were not on the rolls, then there is no way that they could have been Cherokee. That is about the most asinine comment that anyone could say. If you are lulled into thinking that the rolls contained every Cherokee and were conclusive, then you need to back up and start again. The rolls weren't even accurate at many times! It is a historical fact that the Dawes roll contains many errors. From incorrect blood degrees to possible enrollments of some that should not have been enrolled, they are there.

If I am correct, when the Chapman roll of Eastern Cherokee was taken, the enumerator had to physically wonder the Quallatown areas and locate the families to be enrolled. Knowing that this enumerator was coming, how many families conveniently took a walk deeper into the Smokies? I read that the enumerator of this census stated that he would never return to such an area again, as he complained about it being rugged mountain territory. How then could one expect all to have been accounted for? People this is a fact and not speculation. It is also something that we call common sense. You may also want to keep in mind that often times, certain enumerators only counted those of ¼ blood or more as Indian. Thus, this leaves out people who were of mixed Cherokee origins, but were simply not counted as such. This goes back to the question of who can tell you who you are and how much blood does it take to make you Indian.

It is also a historical fact that in order to be enrolled by the Dawes Commission, the individual had to live within a certain area, which was Indian territory. What about those that still resided in Arkansas or surrounding states? They could not enroll, but they were Native American just like their enrolled brothers and sisters. From the time of the removal until the Dawes roll was taken, there was a time span of about 65 years. Do you realize how much moving around one could do in that many years. The Cherokee themselves were known for moving within and without the nation's boundaries. What makes us believe that they all had to stay in one spot?

Now, I realize that we could look at this idea from two perspectives. First of all, we could say that those that left the tribal area did indeed lose their Cherokee *citizenship*. As the laws of the Cherokee Nation stated, that anyone removed themselves and belongings from the tribe's domain, then they would not longer be considered a citizen of the Cherokee Nation. For this reason, they would not be on any future rolls due to that stipulation. However, let us look at it from another view. Even though they moved from the tribe's domain and lost their *citizenship*, they did not and could not lose their *blood ties*. I think that this is where some of the so called genealogists that know everything are lacking in the study of history. Certainly one may have lost their citizenship, but that is not the issue that most of us are dealing with today. We are concerned with blood and not the matter of where they lived.

Along the same subject line, what about those that were enrolled on earlier rolls, but not the Dawes? Are these any less Cherokee than the rest? According to some they are. I cannot find the reasoning behind that, but still the statements are made. Beginning in 1817, there were several rolls taken of the Cherokee including the Reservation rolls, emigration rolls, plus the Henderson, Chapman, Mullay, Siler, Churchill, and Miller, rolls. The Baker roll of 1924 was the final roll of the Eastern Band. These are examples of those east of the Mississippi river. Of course there is the Drennen roll and countless other census records of those living in Indian territory prior to the Dawes roll. So what if one of your ancestors were listed on one or more of these rolls, but didn't reside in Indian territory at the final allotment? Then, you would not be eligible to receive a CDIB and thus, you would not be a citizen of the Cherokee Nation West. Are the descendants of these any less Cherokee than the rest?

I think that this is where the problem begins today when people fail to find their ancestors on the rolls, they immediately assume or are told that their ancestors could not have been Cherokee. That is a very narrow minded statement. What about all of the Cherokee that moved west prior to old settlers? Due to a great earthquake, they moved south into Arkansas to join the old settlers from 1817-1828. There were no records kept of those. What about those that may have remained in the old nation west, when the main body moved into Oklahoma after 1828? Could not many of them intermarried with whites and stayed behind? Could some of them have moved into other states and became lost in a white man's world? I think that you could ask the Cherokee groups in Arkansas and Louisiana about those questions. I am sure that they could give you an answer.

If people are still not convinced that Cherokee moved around, take a look at Sequoyah. As you know, Sequoyah or George Gist, was the inventor of the Cherokee alphabet. It is said that he is buried in Mexico. Now why would a Cherokee end up in Mexico since they couldn't possibly live anywhere but where the tribe was located? I have read countless stories that tell how certain Cherokee, some prominent, moved from the tribe and died in locations all across the country. Suppose there were further offspring before they died. Would those descendants be Cherokee or are they just making it up?

Now here is something to think about. Have you ever considered that there could be people of Cherokee origin living overseas? This goes way back in history, but it is possible. After the first contact, it is a fact that often times Indians were taken as slaves and taken back to European countries or moved to other areas within North America. What if some of those slaves bore children overseas? You would now have a European person trying to tell you that he was of Native American origin from way back. You might immediately call him a liar up front, but was he really lying?

Don't get me wrong, I know that not everyone was Cherokee or any other tribal origin. I also know that not every story of Native American blood in every family is based on fact. However, I think that there is more fact than most give credit for. I just think that those that are genuine are often discounted for some of the reasons that I just discussed. Maybe some are too quick to judge when it comes to another person's heritage.

I realize that I jumped off of the topic at hand a bit, but not really. It was pertinent that I made this point to you during the discussion at hand. After all, you are going to be dealing with rolls and other Indian records if you are researching your Native American heritage. If you run into the problem of not finding them on the rolls, then you need to be aware of what we just discussed. With that in mind, let's proceed with the remainder of this chapter, dealing with finding your tribe.

The above is by no means all the ways that there are to find your roots. The main subject is patience and perseverance! Answers do not come in a day and sometimes they take a life time. If it means a great deal to you, then you will not give up and continue to search. I hope that the above information gives you a good starting point on your search. I wish that I could help people with their family trees, but I cannot.

I know that the above information is somewhat general and cannot possibly be enough to help anyone, but it should give you a good start. Just keep in your mind why you are doing this. It is a tedious job! Researching white records is hard enough when you go back several generations, but wait until you try to search for Indian families that hid their heritage. It is a whole different ball game.

You will see some statements in this book about negative reactions that you may encounter while researching your native roots. I don't wish to discourage you from doing your research, but I only want to warn you about what I came up against. Here is one of the problems that caused me to write the chapter in this book entitled *The Story of Me and Other Things*. Don't expect many people to be impressed with what you are searching for and to jump for joy. This is especially true when dealing with online research. I have met some of the most ruthless, evil people on this thing that they call the Internet. So many folks feel that since they have hid behind the keyboard, that they can be rude to whomever they please. Sometimes I wonder if the Internet should have been invented in the first place. Although, if used properly, you can gain an enormous amount of genealogical information from the use of it. Just be careful.

Now don't think that everyone is going to be hostile towards you just because you are seeking your native roots and you did not grow up on a reservation. You will be surprised at the amount of people that are doing the exact same thing. For whatever reason, seeking Native American roots has just become the *thing* nowadays. As I state in the Chapter concerning *The Story of Me and Other Things*, I began my research long before I knew that this was the case. I was completely surprised at the large amount of people that were seeking to establish their roots within a particular tribe. Granted, Cherokee came up more than any, but almost every tribal entity has a slue of researchers seeking their connections to them.

Don't let this intimidate you. Even if you get rude remarks concerning what we just discussed, keep the faith. It really is no one else's business who your family was or still is. The government tried to rule over the

Native Americans for so long, telling them who they were and weren't. You don't need to let that type of history deter you from finding your roots, being proud of them, and keeping the culture alive. It is the least that we can do.

Now that we have covered some basic ways that you may choose to honor your ancestors, it is time to move on. This next chapter is one that I have to include while we are discussing research and family stories. After that chapter, we will go on to my infamous essay. For now, the following chapter is one that contains a very familiar subject if you have dipped into the realm of Cherokee research. You may have even heard this particular subject mentioned within your own family. If you have not heard of this upcoming subject, get ready, for you will eventually!

Chapter Eight

The Indian Princess Theory

From the title of this chapter, many of you may already know what I am talking about. For those of you who know nothing of this subject, I will gladly explain for you. If you log onto the Internet and begin a search for Cherokee research and genealogy, this term will most assuredly come up. I think that this subject needs to be discussed in this book for the benefit of those who have heard this legend in their own families or for those who need to know about it before beginning their own research.

Let me first begin by explaining the Indian princess story to those who may not know what I am talking about. It is a very common occurrence to hear this used when speaking with someone who states that they are of Cherokee heritage. Most of the time, it is used by those who have heard of their heritage, but know very little about it or the Cherokee themselves. I have heard it before and it comes up in a conversation about Indian heritage and the individual will state that their great grandmother etc., was a Cherokee Indian Princess. Of course, I have also heard this term when dealing with other tribes.

For the record, there has never been any such position of royalty within the Cherokee Nation. As a matter of fact, even the word *Chief* is somewhat deceiving. Most often, that refers to a headman or leader of one of the Cherokee towns. Keep in mind that there was more than one *chief*. Besides the fact that there were chiefs in each of the towns, they were even broken down further than that. You had a peace chief and a war chief. White was the color of the peace chief and red was the color of the war chief. Depending on whether they were at war or not, each one had his own responsibilities. There were also sub-chiefs and other spiritual leaders of the tribe that some may have referred to as chiefs.

Possible Explanations

I want to try to help explain this theory from my own research and experiences. Here again, I am not stating that any of this is etched in stone or the only way to explain it. However, it appears that common sense and historical research backs many of the ideas up. First of all, let's look at the fictional view of this legend or family story. Keep in mind that not all tales of Cherokee or any Indian ancestry are necessarily based on fact, as well as not all are mythical tales made up by family members.

Let's assume that this particular family tale is not true at all, but still the Indian Princess story exists within the family. The family members pass down to their children that there great great grandmother was a Cherokee Indian Princess. The children accept the legend and do not bother to investigate it or the history of the Cherokee themselves. While it is not required that we try to verify our ancestry, it is a must if you are serious about being accepted by other tribal members. Most Native Americans can tell you exactly who their great great grandfather was and where he lived, died, etc. If you walked into a store on the Cherokee Indian reservation and told them how your grandmother was a Cherokee Princess, you would be laughed right off of the boundary, while being called a *twinkie* or *wannabe*.

Let me clarify the above statement a bit further before I go on. I stated above that we are not required to verify our ancestry. If you really get down to it, I guess that you could say that by trying to verify what your grandmother told you, it would appear as if you did not trust or believe her. I know why we do the research and that is fine, but have we ever looked at it that way before? My grandmother has been dead for 25 years and I miss her dearly. If she were alive and told me something like the

Indian Princess theory, I would most definitely believe her. There is no man on this Earth that could convince me to tell her to her face that I had to go verify it before I could believe her. No matter how ignorant the remark may seem to others, it would be gospel to me coming from her. Mainly, because I know what type of lady she was and how honest she was.

Granted, honest people can make honest mistakes. That is the only justification that I can find for trying disprove what a loved one says to you. I know for a fact that my own grandmother would have not intentionally lied to me or anyone else for all of the money in the world. I have been told by some that I did not personally know, that she had. Needless to say, those people might as well have struck me in the face with an ax handle. I know that this is not a book about who is and who is not honest, but I had to explain myself. At this point, you can see that I like to write as I speak. I will try to not go off on too many tangents and lose you along the way!

Going back to our first example, we can see that an erroneous family legend was passed down by the parents to the children. From there, it could continue for many generations until someone forgets or simply does the research. Just because you hear that you have Indian ancestry, does not mean that you have to drop what you are doing and go research. It all depends on what you want to do with it. If you want to pursue tribal membership and the serious study of your heritage, then the research is inevitable.

Now, let us look at Indian Princess theory from a factual standpoint. I have heard many explanations for this phenomena, but I tend to stick with the following a bit more should there be fact to the story. You must first remember that unless you are Native American, you have some other heritage in your past. Until the white man came to this country, there were only the first people. With that in mind, you must know that Europeans probably defined or explained things much differently than the Native Americans did. Where the daughter of a chief was simply that to the

Natives, the same girl was called a princess by those of European descent. Basically, the meaning is still the same. It is just that the terminology might not fit the Native American vocabulary very well.

So it is possible that your Indian Princess was indeed a daughter of a headman or chief. She may have not been called that by her own people, but those of European descent knew no other way to describe her. Since they were use to the concept of Kings, Queens, and such, it only made sense to them. If this was the case, then your family legend may have more truth to it than you think. Here again, only research could reveal the truth if you so desire to locate it. If you do not wish to question your family, then you do not have to if quiet pride is all that you desire. Just remember that if you wish to go any further, the research will have to be done.

Another explanation of this theory that I have heard of involves the fact that in the early days of the settlers, some were captured by the Indians and adopted into the tribes. Maybe a female was taken captive and eventually adopted by the town chief. From that point, she was his daughter. It is interesting to note that particularly in Cherokee homes, some were called brother, sister, etc. that were not. If they were members of the same clan and were living with another family for one reason or another, they may very well be called a family member. In accordance with the old ways, they were family. If this was the case, maybe your ancestor lived with a chief or headman and his family. From that point, she became known as his daughter even though there were no direct blood ties. This makes a genealogical nightmare come true when trying to place her with the correct set of parents if you have no other leads!

There are probably other explanations for this family legend that is so common in Cherokee research. I can't speak for the other tribes, but I assure you that there are probably similar stories. An interesting point here is the fact that besides the princess story, the Cherokee tribe is the most common tribal entity that lineage is claimed from. This is particularly true in the southeastern US. The Cherokee were one of the largest and most well known tribes in this area. Once encompassing eight southern states, you could say that they were definitely a powerful nation.

When you mention the word Indian in North Carolina, the word Cherokee just comes up naturally. When someone in this area speaks of Indian ancestry, it is almost always Cherokee. While this may be the case, there were more than one tribe in this area. Many are not aware of the Catawba, Cheraw, Sara, Keyowee, Saponi, Occaneechi, Eno, Tuscarora, Sugarees, Waxhaw, or Saxaphahaw. Many people may have actually descended from one of these tribes as opposed to the Cherokee. However, the ability to research some of these tribes are much more difficult, if not impossible, to accomplish.

In summary of this chapter, let's review the basics. First of all, you can see that many people have similar legends in their families. The Indian Princess Theory is the most prevalent in Cherokee research. The question is whether you are going to research the legend and prove or disprove it. You can also see that the mere mention of this theory can bring labels upon yourself and your family's heritage. Should this discourage you from doing research? I would hope not, but I have found that it does to many people. Out of fear of being laughed at, many tend to ignore their heritage due to the Indian Princess story being told to them. I would hope that my explanations of the legend would help reassure those that may be considering abandoning their research.

Just because your family told you that you have an ancestor that was an Indian princess, does not mean that they were not Indian. She might not have been a princess, but that is all. Your ancestor could very well fall into one of the factual explanations of this theory. On the other hand, it may all fall apart on you. It is entirely up to you whether you wish to pursue it. In conclusion, I must reiterate that if you wish to proceed deeper into your history, then you will have to seek the truth. Above all, remember those before you.

Chapter Nine

The Story of Me and Other Things

The following chapter contains the essay that I have already mentioned to you several times in this book. This is the one that was published on my heritage web site for so long. I have edited it somewhat, but the basic story is still the same. I use some silly examples throughout this chapter, so try to bear with me as I proclaim my gospel to you! I like to write as I talk, so you can imagine what type of public speaker that I am. I think that you will enjoy this chapter if you will just keep an open mind and hear me out. Now on to the original essay as you may have seen before on the Internet:

Hello and Osiyo (In Cherokee): My name is Brian Voncannon and I am a full time law enforcement officer. I spend my spare time either writing, making handmade crafts, or working out. I sell my artwork on consignment basis at a local store. I don't make a living doing that, but simply do these things because I enjoy them. Many members of my immediate family are members of state recognized Indian tribes. Most of us have carried a pride amongst ourselves for many generations of our heritage. Particularly on the Lambert side of my family. I have recently, in the last 3 years, made our lineage public. Sometimes, I wish that I never had as my family warned me about. As you read on, you will find out why. And before you think it has something to do with racism, it is exactly the opposite of that. Anyway, I began a study of my family and the Cherokee. I also worked on other branches of the family, but the Lamberts are the closest to me, as my grandmother was by maiden name.

Before I go any further, please understand that I am not speaking ill of any one person, nor am I trying to disrespect anyone personally. I have been personally offended by some folks with real good communication skills. When I mention full bloods, mixed bloods, CDIB carriers, state or federal recognition, etc. it is for the purpose of getting my point across. I am not on a crusade to help destroy anyone, overthrow the government or anything like that. I am not speaking ill of anyone who is a member of a federally or state recognized tribe, nor any of the unrecognized tribes, as many Indian people do not carry a membership card at all. That still doesn't change their heritage. Member cards haven't been around that long anyway.

This essay is in defense of those who are proud of their heritage and have been labeled as a whole. I am not defending those who have purposely made fools of themselves and asked to be called names. Those are the ones who have created the problems today for the rest. I care about this country and have served the flag proudly in the U.S. Army. I have my own opinions on many things, as that is my freedom. No, no one died and left me the boss nor am I a representative of all living things, nor am I some type of authority on these subjects. I am doing something that I normally do not do and that is express my opinions a bit more harsh than normal.

I usually keep my mouth shut, even in the face of rude comments, as arguing does not solve anything. It is okay to speak one's mind, but you must use good judgment when doing so. Am I trying to insult anyone person in this paper? No. In some instances in this essay, I mention the term new ager and many others. If this is what you consider your religion or practice, then that is your freedom of choice. In America, you have the right to believe as you please. So, just respect my opinions and I will respect yours to the best of my ability.

Some things that I have done to honor my heritage involved creating web sites, talking with other people, making trips to court houses, and contacting other researchers on the Internet. I had no idea at the time, that so many people were trying research their native roots. Some were simply trying to see if they had any Indian blood at all from scratch. When I started mentioning what I was doing, some of the people lit up like you'd tossed a match in their gas tank. The mere mention of Indian blood research and my pride in such, just fired some people up. I was not prepared for this. They practically wanted to start examining my family tree, my teeth, my mating habits, my DNA, and my eye color to try to find a smidgen of truth in what I was saying. Good gosh! I doubt that some of them could have yelled any louder at me than if you'd made them chew on tin foil with a mouthful of dental fillings.

People whom I didn't know, wanted to see my *papers* or my *card* and the pedigree to go along with it before they would even consider that my family just might be telling the truth. I thought, "what am I, a mixed breed poodle or something?" Do you want to know if I have had my shots also? Am I AKC registered? I really didn't argue with anyone about it, but took some serious offense as to what they were saying. What was going on here? I don't remember ever eating Christmas dinner with these folks, nor waking up to find them eating my eggs and calling me "cousin". These were people that just knew all about me.

Now, it wasn't like I was trying to proclaim to them that I was something like the one and only true medicine man that descended from the chief of the Ugabooga tribe. I just told them what I had been raised with and how it came to be. That just made it worse. I figured that there is something going on in society today that I was not aware of. I knew right then, that I had been in the woods too long about this and needed to find out why people treated me the way that they did and still do. In any rate, I continued my study and kept the pride that my mother and grandmother taught me to have, while examining the current situation in order to find out why this sparked such a flame.

Because of the above, I have been called a wannabe, money seeker, scam artist, liar, yarn spinner, and a few other names that I would rather not mention. Of course, those comments, though made to me, are basically directed at my ancestors by people who have never met me nor my family. At first, I could not understand what the term "wannabe" really meant until I started doing some reading on the Internet. I found out that certain types of people have basically created a stereotype for the rest of us.

Not only are Indians themselves stereotyped by many people as having to wear *war bonnets* and say "*how*" when they meet, all Indian women being called *squaws* (actually can be quite offensive), and that every Indian is this super type of spiritual person who is born with an innate knowledge of how to do sacred ceremonies, etc. Oh yes, and all Indians look like the ancient Plains Indians. They cannot be any of a lighter complexion nor can they make it through a day without eating Buffalo or show an inability to speak English. Don't laugh, some people think that. I wonder if some of these people get confused when they go to the Qualla Boundary and can't seem to locate the teepees?

As I stated above, I did not really understand the concept of *wannabe*, *twinkie*,etc. until I started getting into the mainstream of Native American research. I guess I could not understand why some full bloods or some members of the federally recognized tribes would not accept a mixed blood's or non federally enrolled person's loyalty to his or her heritage without labeling them. As I said, some and not all. Anyway, I found out that it seems a few have helped get most of us labeled and from hearing what I have, there is no wonder. I began doing some searching on the Internet for many different tribes and the people that were claiming to belong to them (non-CDIB carriers). There are literally thousands of people seeking their native roots these days, so finding someone doing so, is quite easy. Now here again, I am *not* talking about everyone. I am hitting on those few or many that have made it hard on the rest.

Federal Recognition

In case some of you do not know, a CDIB card is a certificate of degree of Indian blood or the white card. This card is obtained by applying to one of the Federally recognized tribes. In essence, it states your Indian *blood quantum*. The Cherokee Nation membership card, separate from the CDIB is a blue card. For further information on the aspects of registration, visit the Cherokee Nation's web site located at http://www.cherokee.org/. *Blood quantum* is actually a government imposed term that refers to the amount of Indian blood that flows in your veins.

Before the days of government rolls, allotments, etc., I don't think anyone knew what that meant. You either were or you weren't. Federal recognition of tribes falls under the Dept. of the Interior, Bureau of Indian Affairs. Tribes will have a local office and agents assigned to that particular area or tribe. A tribe is a sovereign entity with some of it's assets held in trust by the federal government. For example, the Eastern Band of Cherokee live on a reservation of about 56,000 acres, spread out over a 5 county area in North Carolina. The lands belong to the tribe and it's members, but is held in trust by Uncle Sam. Looking back over history, you can see that this domain is no where near what it used to be. Now, how did that happen?

I did not decide to *become Indian* one day. I did not fabricate Indian ancestry because I wanted to be in with a group, nor did I begin my study because so many other people were doing it. I began my study before I even knew that people cared about that part of their heritage. I did not grow up on a reservation and I don't claim to know all the problems associated with that. My study of my heritage began about 3 years ago (my heritage began when I was born) when I met a Cheyenne woman at my church. She was speaking to our congregation at the First Baptist Church of Locust, NC as she was a missionary to her own people on the tribal lands. While speaking, she told how proud she was of her heritage and how God had blessed her with such a family. At that moment, I realized that I had been neglecting to learn more about my lineage, which was taught to me since I was a boy of about 7 or 8 years old. For the record, I am a big *31* now! I knew all of my life what I had been taught, but just never dug deep into the history of a proud people. I discovered much that I didn't know as I looked for all of the *hidden Indians* in my family tree as someone once put it to me.

Do I know everything about *being* Indian or anything for that matter? Of course not! No one does. Is there a book out there that you can buy that will give you Indian lessons? Absolutely not. Do I expect everyone to agree with every aspect of this page? If I think that they will, then I guess there have been no lessons learned thus far on my part. People really do stereotype Indians today though. As a person of mixed Indian ancestry, you may or may not *look* Indian according to some people's standards. Who is the one who sets standards on looks anyway? Anyone who has studied genetics, knows about Gregor Mendel. I studied a good bit on him and his work when I was in pre-med. (no, I'm not a doctor, but was once going to school to be one). Traits will show up when and where they want to. Someone of mixed ancestry may not have the looks that television taught Americans to think is the way all Indians look. Oh, that word *television*. That is another story when it comes to stereotyping.

I have heard some people say that they get sick of seeing all of the *white Indians* dancing at powwows and walking around claiming their heritage. What about those members of the Cherokee Nation and the Eastern Band that don't *look Indian* according to these same people's standards? I have looked at many rolls of the Eastern Cherokee and at the Dawes roll on numerous occasions. As a matter of fact, I have the Dawes roll of the Five Civilized tribes scanned onto a CD-ROM. Now, when I look at some of the blood quantums that were there, now about 100 years ago, it makes me start to think. As you may know, the Dawes roll is what the Cherokee Nation West uses as their basic member requirement.

In other words, to qualify for membership, you must be a DIRECT descendant of someone who was enrolled by the Dawes commission. Okay, suppose you locate your great grandfather on the Cherokee by Blood section of the Dawes roll. He is listed as being 1/32 Cherokee. You now have met the basic member requirement, but not all. By the way, your ancestors had to be living in what was then called Indian Territory for them to have been enrolled on this roll.

So, you learn that your great grandfather married a white woman and the family eventually moved back to North Carolina, and thus, you came to be. There were no further intermarriages with any of Indian ancestry. What is your blood quantum now? It should be 1/256th Cherokee. Well, you get your CDIB and finally, your membership in the Cherokee Nation. You are now a federally recognized Indian without ever living on a reservation. If you don't think that this case is possible, ask around. There are members of federal tribes that do not live within the tribes boundaries. My cousin has a good friend who is a member of the Eastern Band, but lives somewhere in south Georgia. All right, by now, you have blonde hair and blue eyes because of intermarriages and simple genetics. As a matter of fact, some may not know that you were enrolled unless you told them. What if you decided that you wanted to dance at a powwow? That's great, so you go for it. Well, along comes someone whom you over hear saying how it makes them sick watching those wannabes and white people out there pretending to be Indian, talking about you! Would a statement like that make even a federally enrolled Indian mad? You bet it would! Did the person make the statement based on what you looked like physically or because that you did not grow up on a reservation? Maybe if you checked that persons' card, they might be the same blood quantum, more or even less.

Do I think that the person who grew up on the reservation had a harder life than the other? More than likely, they did. That certainly is a factor to consider, but does it change actual blood? I guess here is where you can get into a long discussion on who should and who should not be Indian, depending on the lifestyle and not simple blood ties to the nation. As in all things, that is still another matter of opinion. Now what if the 1/256 Cherokee that I mentioned above was not qualified to enroll, but had Cherokee blood that he or she was aware of from one source or another? Would they be any less Cherokee? What about those who did not reside within the territory during the Dawes Act? Are these people non-Cherokee also?

I realize that there has to be standards in the case of federal tribes. I am also sure that they are totally aware that there are Cherokee who do not meet the requirements to enroll in the Nation. If everyone who was the least bit Cherokee were allowed to enroll, I think that they may have an administrative nightmare on their hands! I am not saying that anything should be changed as I have no right to suggest it. That is not what I am getting at. The fact is that, as in my example, people themselves, want to be able to say who is and who is not able to claim their heritage. Sometimes, I hate to use the word, *claim*. It almost sounds like you are seeking money when you say it. Maybe I should use the word, *proclaim* instead. I still say that all of this goes back to some people making it hard on the rest. It appears that people have gotten away from what I heard a Cherokee Councilman say once on a video entitled *Cherokee*. He said that Cherokee heritage was passed down and that only one of your ancestors need be Cherokee for that to be the case. He said that long ago, it was decided that if you were Cherokee, then your kids would be Cherokee too and so on.

More on Looks

When you go to a powwow, be it intertribal, Cherokee, or whatever tribe is hosting it, you will be amazed if you are somewhat narrow minded when it comes to what an Indian is supposed to look like according to stereotypes. You may see someone with blue eyes, red hair, or blonde hair dancing in the circle. Are they all full bloods? No, but they have Indian ancestry, unless some non-Indians slip in somehow. You will see tall people, short people, etc. Other than the dancers in their regalia, you will see Indians wearing shorts, T-shirts, blue jeans and tennis shoes. Why aren't they all wearing their war bonnets? Why did you hear a few of them talking about the new movie that came out the other day? Why weren't they all talking in another language? Why weren't they all drunk and whooping it up? After all, that's what a pow-wow is isn't it? Most of these questions have been asked before and many to me. Let me tell you that the word *regalia* is the proper term for the dancer's outfit and not costume.

Still hitting on the blood quantum and looks a bit. Did you know how much Cherokee blood that Chief John Ross had? He was about 1/8. From the pictures that I have seen of him, he might not fit your stereotype of what a Cherokee was supposed to look like. When you think about it, would some of the Cherokees from the past be able to meet the member requirements of some tribes today? I don't' have a CDIB and I'm really not worried about that too much. My girlfriend of five years, is currently tracing her Cherokee genealogy from Oklahoma and as it looks, she may very well qualify for one. By the way, she lives near Charlotte, North Carolina. I've already mentioned this, but her family moved away from the tribe about the time of the Dawes roll and ended up back in North Carolina somehow, but she still has relatives in Oklahoma.

Her great grandmother, raised her father since his mother was young. He called her *momma* all of his life and learned a great deal from her. She taught him about making flutes, and other traditional things that she knew about. She would not teach him about herbal medicine, as she said that was only for the girls. One big thing that she told him, was to keep his heritage to himself. She wasn't ashamed, and neither is my girlfriend's dad, but she told him how he would be treated if he let others know of his ancestry. This was back in the late 1940's, early 50's. I have seen pictures of her and there is no doubt of her ancestry; however, she is listed as white on all documents here in North Carolina. Imagine that? I guess that she could not possibly have been Cherokee due to that factor right? Wrong. Does that change the pride that her family has today that was hidden for so long? No. Does that make them any less Indian? No, but I am sure that would still create a debate among some as I talked about earlier.

Is this family trying to get money or are they trying to embellish their stories to make family life more interesting? Of course not. No, she didn't tell him that she was a Cherokee princess. She taught him about life as she knew it. Will you say harsh words to this man also? In fact, speaking ill of this man's grandmother is a sure trip to the hospital. She was practically his mother and everything about her is a cherished memory, including the Indian blood which still flows in his veins. When down grading his family for moving back to NC and accusing them of *selling out* or calling him a wannabe for wanting to learn more of his heritage today, you open up a real can of worms. You are talking about real people who are no longer alive to defend themselves, plus you are trying to destroy those that are here that have to listen to it.

Some More Origins of the Dreaded Wannabe Title

While I am on the subject of powwows, I want to express some things I learned about them. Yes, I attend powwows. I've already covered them, but just wanted to express some things that I learned why attending these events. I remember about a year ago at a powwow I was attending in North Carolina, what the MC, John Blackfeather Jeffries said before the Grand Entry. He started out by welcoming all who were there, native and white. He explained a brief history of the powwow and what it was for. He also stated that we were not there to entertain anyone. The dancers were there to honor their respective tribes and otherwise, we were there to have fellowship with one another. He said that if we gave the idea that we were trying to entertain, then we needed to apologize for that is not what it was about. People were told specifically when they could and could not take pictures, but that request was ignored. They were told not to take any photographs when the circle was being blessed by an older gentleman who happened to be Apache. Still, people took pictures.

People were asked to not throw their trash on the grounds, but still they did it. By the way, some of the litter bugs were Indian also. Does that fit the typical stereotype of all Indians looking at the trash on the ground with a tear in their eyes? Many do believe in taking care of the land, but Indians are people and not some type of fairy tale out of a children's book.

What am I getting at? Things such as these all add up in the realm of Native America. Combine disrespect like that with other things and pretty soon, resentment takes effect. When some of the people who did these things later tell one of the dancers, "oh, I'm Indian too", do you think that they are going to want to hear that? No, the person has probably just got himself labeled as a twinkie or a wannabe. There is no wonder that some people just don't have a chance because of how others act. I know of a person who is not Indian, but loves the spiritual side of the Native American. I am not real close to this person, but I know them. The conversation came up that I was of Indian ancestry somehow when we were talking about our families. Anyway, when this person heard this, they immediately started asking me for advice on things like: what types of herbs are the best to smudge with, how they had a dream catcher and wondered if I would bless it for them? I thought sure, I'll just wave my arms and murmur the secret words. Now, that seemed a bit foolish don't you think?

This person thought that just because I had Indian ancestry that all of this stuff came naturally to me and that I had been taught, as all Indians are(?),all of the spiritual ways. If I went up to my friend who is 1/2 Cherokee and asked him to bless my dream catcher and empower a crystal for me, he would laugh me six ways to Sunday. When this person asked me this question, I didn't know what to say, but "What?" I then knew that I had met one of those people that was making it hard on many of us. This person, who admitted to not having any Indian blood, was one of those people who have sought after the spiritual teachings of our forefathers and tried to fabricate it into their own religion. I will tell you that I am Southern Baptist and am a born again Christian. I know that my ancestors worshipped a bit differently from the way I do, and some still worship that way today, but I respect that history. I am not a teacher nor a student of Cherokee medicine nor any other old way and have never claimed to be. I can however recognize someone who turns my stomach and no doubt turns the stomachs of those who do worship by traditional means. Geez...I see more and more where this has come from.

Let Me Introduce Myself

I am not a full blood Indian. I am what some will call a mixed blood, breed, Brunswick stew or whatever the going terms are now. What did I learn growing up about being Indian or *part Indian*. Which part, my hand or my foot, as most will say? I learned that people would treat you bad at one time and even still some today if you told them that you had Indian blood in your veins. I learned about the problems that Indians face, as everyone else does. Even in my own family, I learned what alcoholism, poverty, Diabetes, arthritis were. I myself am afflicted with the later. Oh, has no one ever told you about those things? Check the census records and see if they are there. If they are not, then they must not have existed, right?

I learned to respect my elders, not to waste anything, and to be honest. I learned from my great grandfather, that land is valuable and will pay for itself through what it yields. My mother taught me that the killing of animals was for clothes and food only. If I had both, then I was not to kill. No, the excuse of wanting a deer head on the wall like my friends wasn't good enough for her. I learned to love the mountains and spend a good deal of time on the Qualla Boundary, which my great grandfather spent much of his time. I learned that there were things in the natural world that cannot be explained and must only be accepted. I learned that nature has produced things that can help heal us and I learned about the rivers from stories about grandpa Lambert. I won't explain that one, as those of you who know, will just know. I learned to hold dear to me, things that others may consider waste. Other than that, I grew up wearing T-shirts and blue jeans. I drove several broken down cars, which I still do today, and did things as every normal boy does. Most of all, I learned that God created us all. It doesn't matter who you are, where you live, we are all His children.

Two Kinds

I have found, in my cyber-travels, earthly experiences, etc., that there are two different types of people who proclaim their heritage(?) proudly or are searching for it. Those who are genuine and those who are not. Some of these people are the ones who may or may not have Indian ancestry and are seeking to establish it, or find it, for whatever reason. This is fine, but with some, it doesn't stop there. Sounds okay so far. Well, here is where it all goes down the toilet. Some, again I say only some, will begin to contact the tribes via email or post messages at the tribal web site like you will see below. Again, sounds okay so far, but hold on. It probably would be okay except for the messages start to sound like this in some cases. The names have been changed to protect the innocent. Just kidding with that part. This is more real than you think. Please, no offense meant to anyone, this is just an example of what is happening....for real:

To: The X Tribe of Blah Blah
From: Thundering Raccoon Chasing the Lightning or Mary
Ref: My tribal heritage
Dear Chief Whoever,
    "How!" You can call me Mary. I found out yesterday, from a friend, that I am part Indian. Since yesterday, I have learned much. As I sat under the moon, the spirits of my newly found people gave my Indian name to me and told me to seek knowledge from you. Yes you! I am on a quest for knowledge and wish to become one with nature. I am writing you to see if you can teach me "the ways". I know this is my path. I have recently started up a chapter of "save the ground hog" in my neighborhood and have also gone door to door asking for Styrofoam cups. We must work together to save the Earth! By the

way, my 16th great grandmother was Jane Whoevershewas. Can you do my genealogy for me? I know that you will know of her because she was your tribal Princess in 1600. I am awaiting your call under the stars. 1-800-fry-bread or email me at howlingthunder@rocketboy.com.

That's one type. Now here is another of the extreme letters, which deals with those who are not Indian, admit it, but wish to follow the "ways" as they may call it:

To: Chief Whatever
From: Bloody Pickle in the Spring Time or Eugene
Ref: The true ways
How!
You don't know me and I'm not Indian, but I have a deep respect for you people. I feel bad about what the Europeans did to you guys and I just want to take this time to apologize on their behalf. I know you people can't make it on your own two feet, make decisions, or just be plain human, so you will need as much pity as possible. Even though I am not Indian, I am a member of the "Native American Church" I am so glad that I learned about what you guys worship. My life is so much more complete now. I met a medicine man on the Internet, here in New York, and he was sending out literature about his services. I was a bit skeptical at first, due to his high prices, but I am glad that I signed up. I am now a student of "the ways" (wink :) You know what I am talking about! Everyday, I do just like you Indians do, I go outside every morning and become one with my brain. I can see much more clearly now. I just wish that I had some Indian blood in me to make it more sacred. I know that this stuff comes natural to you guys, so you'll have to bear with me while I learn. My medicine teacher, Jim Scamsmybutt, says that pretty soon, I will be ready to teach others. He adopted me the other day into his tribe over the Internet. I know you have heard of us, we are the Gonnagetya Tribe. We are recognized by the Official Association of Medicine Men of Iraq. As soon as I save up the $150,000, I am going to get my certification to teach "the ways". I hope to go and meet my teacher someday, but

due to the "old ways", he cannot tell me exactly where he lives. You know all about that don't you, brother? Anyway, I was starting to get tired of playing with this tribe, and I was wondering if you could adopt me as a member of yours? I figured you could use a good medicine man in the tribe. After all, with all of the scams out there, it is good to have someone who REALLY knows what the old ways were like!!

Okay, these were extreme and do not represent the majority. On the other hand, you might see a posting or letter like the one below:

To: Mr. Smith, Chief of the X Tribe
From: Billy
Ref.: Seeking my Heritage
Greetings:
  I visited your tribe's web site and found it most informative. I am a descendant of an intermarriage between an Indian woman and my 4th great grandfather. My family told me that they were of your tribe. I am trying to find more information about them and my heritage as I am proud of who I am and who they were. I have visited some of your powwows and really enjoyed it. I think it is bad that people allow so great a heritage to be hidden or simply slip it under the rug. I feel that it is my job to carry it on and one day, pass all of the information along to my children. If you can steer me in the right direction, I would be most appreciative.

Okay, the first two letters are obviously full of bull. I don't care if they descended from the first Chief and his two sisters, they are full of it. Their letters are foolish and are a complete embarrassment to themselves. They make a mockery of the culture and the second letter explains how not only was a non- Indian fellow stealing the culture, but the poor guy was being ripped off. If he was that stupid, he deserved to have his money taken. The last letter was appropriate, polite, and genuine. It did not go over the limit, nor did it make a fool of the sender.

Folks, who from the above, would you think *deserved* to be called wannabe or twinkie or whatever? The first two, right? Sure. I know that you may not think so, but I have seen the last example labeled that way also. Oh yes. Why? Probably because of the first two types of people. These examples are not as made up as you would think them to be. As a matter of fact, some of my ideas for the funny examples came from real posts that I have seen. The last letter is probably the most common and I do not see anything wrong with it. I cannot defend the first two people at all, they earned the title. The last guy, is probably as genuine as you can tell from just an email. No, he obviously isn't enrolled anywhere. He shows respect and is simply interested in learning of his heritage for real reasons.

If you slammed the third guy, you would do more damage than you think. First of all, you would probably spook him from wanting to mention his heritage anymore. He would then stereotype *you* and think that all Indians will treat him that way. Would they? Probably not. The first two types of people have ruined it for everyone else. Because of them, if you are blonde headed, blue eyed, and live in a big city, there is no way for you to mention your heritage without being labeled. I realize that families that left the tribal area for whatever reason, may be looked upon by some of the tribe members with animosity. I have heard their actions called, "selling out" in order to get a better life. Anger arises for those who hid their heritage in order for their kids or themselves to get a better chance at things the white man already had. I can understand that anger, but I cannot change the past. I wasn't alive then and it doesn't change my DNA, blood, or pride.

Could there be embellished stories that contain no truth to them in families? Sure. Anything is possible. Does that make everyone's story the same? No. I realize that there are story tellers in all families, especially long ago when there were no TVs. Do I think that some people may have tried to scam the government and get money on the Guion Miller Roll? I am sure that happened, but I cannot tell you who they were. As a law enforcement officer, I have learned that dishonesty in this world is quite frequent. But still, not everyone. Did my direct family try to get money on that roll?

No, but some cousins did; however, there claim was a totally different line that I did not descend from. My great grandfather was an honest, Christian man, whom loved his family and worked hard all of his life as a farmer. Had he never mentioned our blood, his actions would have led someone to think that there was something different about him.

Real Indians

Do I know any *real* Indians? (with humor) Well, knowing what I think of that definition, I will still say… yes. Some friends and acquaintances of mine are Lumbee, Cherokee, Choctaw, Monacan, Abenaki, Occaneechi and more. A good friend of mine is 1/2 Cherokee. We have known each other for a long time and have gone fishing, *hung out* and done other things that normal people do. No, he doesn't live on a reservation. As a matter of fact, he is quite economically challenged where he lives. I talked a gun out of his father's hand one night when he wanted to kill himself. The alcoholism and family problems got to him. Sounds like real problems that real people have doesn't it? Anyway, neither one of us has ever asked to see each other's membership cards. I guess I could ask him if it would be all right to scan his father's card onto the Internet so everyone could verify this story, huh? Wrong.

While in the United States Infantry Training Center -US Army, Fort Benning, Georgia, my best friend was a full blood from out west. Notice that I did not say which tribe. It is because I never asked him as it didn't matter. His first name was Lester, and if you are reading this Lester, it would be nice to hear from you again. Whoa! (an 11 Bravo thing) Now some will probably want to say, "oh my, here is another wannabe trying to hang out with Indians so he can become one." You can print it in your history books that is not the case.

Growing up, our lineage or our race was never mentioned or worried about for that matter. We just knew that we were friends and that is all that mattered. I didn't say, "wait a minute, before I can accept you as an Indian or as a friend, I will need to check your card and verify that your family isn't a bunch of liars". Had I done that, we would not be friends at all. Had they did that to me, we would probably not be friends, because it shows that you have no respect for other's families nor do you have a good way of presenting yourself as a human being.

Do I understand why labels have been attached to such people as mentioned here in this essay? Absolutely. It doesn't matter what area of life you are looking at. There is always a select few that create problems for the rest. Then those take on a band of followers and pretty soon, it looks like the whole bunch is rotten. Is there anything that I can do to change this whole situation? No. It will probably get worse before it gets better. Of course, one day when people get tired of it all, another idea will take it's place. Those with genuine hearts, will know no rest. Probably only time will show.

One more point here that I feel has created some stereotyping of *white Indians*…Indian names. Yes, many people have these. Long ago, an Indian name was the person's name. It normally stated something about their persona or some important event. They may have had several throughout their life times, maybe one at birth, another when they became adults, and maybe another if an important event warranted a new name. In any rate, it was sacred. A person's name is not to be disrespected. Do all people of Indian ancestry have Indian names? Probably not, but some do. Some may have been given one by their family or a respected elder of the tribe. If you really want to know what my true Indian name is…it is Brian. If there is something that my mother has called me, you probably don't want to know what that one is!

Now here comes the problem that has helped get many non recognized Indians get a bad rap. Some folks have acquired Indian names by some means and have caused some real anger between them and some other families. For example, if you met someone like the goof balls in the letters that I made up, and one of them told you that his or her Indian name was the same as your 4th great grandfather's whom died on the trail of tears, you would get mad. They might not have known that, but you would get mad. I have heard tale of some non Indians who seek Native spirituality methods, taking Indian names. Some of these names are historically attached to prominent Indian people. I take that as an insult and then some. Many times, and here again not all, you will see romantic names such as, "Whispering Water Swan" or "Master of the Wind Spirits", etc. I made these up, but maybe someone is using them?

Genuine Tribes and the Scam Artists

Some final thoughts on what I think of all the Cherokee or other tribal groups out there who are not recognized and those who would be called scam artists. I think that these should be treated as anything else in this world. If someone is not obviously hurting you and committing a crime, then why not leave them alone? In my opinion, many fraudulent tribes and groups can be spotted a mile away and of course, some may not be. More than likely, if we did not know what the word *money* was, then there would be less trouble in this area and other aspects of life.

Certainly, there are probably people, as my made up example in one of the letters above, who are obviously trying to take people for what they are worth. However, just because a private group needs money to run their affairs does not make them frauds. When I talk about spotting a fraud a mile away, I mean something like the example that is used in the following paragraph.

Suppose you meet a fellow over the notorious Internet (this thing has caused some problems over the years), who says he is a chief of some unknown tribe. He says that he is out recruiting members who descended from this tribe or anyone of Indian blood in order to start up a new tribe. He promises that they are going to get land, and that an intent to petition for federal recognition has been filed for his new tribe. He states that he wants to hold onto the old ways and give everyone a chance to belong that deserves to. In return for membership and all of the bells and whistles that he mentioned, you will need to send him a fee of $250 for enrollment. He says that he doesn't require applications, only a letter with a money order. Oh, leave the "pay to" section blank. He explains this by stating that the tribal checking account is not yet ready and their may be some slight changes in the way they are going to be printed. His market will no doubt be the people who just don't meet the requirements for enrollment, but want to pursue tribal membership. Okay, he's got their attention. Finally, someone who will accept me, right?

Well, the story goes on. Keep in mind, this is another one of my parables, but with a truthful meaning and lesson involved. Anyway, this so called chief has gotten his claws into what could be a very sincere person who is just proud of their heritage, but *disenfranchised*. Now, he leads his victim and many others like him or her, out for the kill. This chief, as he calls himself, convinces all of his new followers (in his chat room) that he is some kind of chosen one and needs money to really get the tribe going. As I said before, legitimate people do need money to do things also. However, this guy might ask his members for large amounts of cash to be sent to his tribal office. This tribal office might or might not exist. Anyway, the people have never seen him and should never send money to him anyway. After he tries to earn their respect and their money, he skips town. Now you have a few or a whole bunch of people who can't seem to locate their chief or their money. Sound crazy? It can and does happen.

What was wrong with the picture above? Well, from a law officers point of view, I see what we call a Bunco artist. I think I spelled that right. You could call him a real scam artist who has taken people with a criminal intent. Other than the fact that this is a common criminal, he has defamed the tribal name, and created an embarrassing situation for those involved. It is called, learning the hard way. What clues did this guy give that gave away his identity as a criminal? At first, you just didn't know. To the unsuspecting person, or to one who is just hungry to belong to a tribe, it sounds just wonderful. Now I can be a member of a tribe, carry a member card, look forward to going to powwows on our own land and everything! Oh buyer beware! Some of those folks who would have written letters like the ones above in my examples, will probably fall into this category.

As I said, to some people who do not understand how things are today, this might seem like an opportunity. The chief has offered to accept you into the tribe, made some nice promises to you, and most of all he has become your friend! Of course he has become your friend! Now for some more clues that you should be aware of. First of all, beware of who you meet over the Internet. I have met some super nice people on the net, but I have met some real *whackos* too. The victims of this scam should have started to worry when they met this guy. Here he is, a chief who has no people. Who made him chief? Was he elected or simply erected? This should have been a big clue. Now, he asks for money early on in the introduction. The first thing that this guy probably told the people was to send him some money. He is basically selling tribal memberships and at a real bargain...$250! Wow, is that all? What a guy!

After the money speech, he has to convince the people that they will be getting their money's worth. He told them about future tribal lands with this and that. He also won their confidence by telling them that his tribe has already filed for federal petition. Actually, it is probably more like sent a letter of intent to petition. Anyone can do that. It really doesn't hold water. Filing the actual petition is good, but even then, it is up to Uncle Sam if it was good enough. So, the unsuspecting person, who knows little of what they are doing, has been suckered. Now the person thinks that he has a tribal card coming in the mail, future land holdings, a CDIB in the works, and is a close personal friend of the chief. Heck, they may even get to be a council member! Well, weeks go by and by, but no tribal card or thank you letter. These people are now left empty in their hearts and their wallets. The guy on the other end? I am sure that he felt some remorse as he cashed all of those blank money orders.

Lesson number one is be careful and know what is going on before you jump into the river of life. Things like the above happen for real. Maybe not tribal fraud, but I have personally investigated rip off artists who have taken people for thousands of dollars. They are everywhere and not just in the realm of Indian tribes or clubs. Lesson two is know who you are dealing with. This is where recognized tribes are much safer, I hope. At least you know that they are real. Anyone can start up a club or what they call a tribe. They don't have to be Native American. I could start up the *Super Secret Cherokee Rifle Club* tomorrow and it have nothing to do with being Cherokee nor have any member requirements. I could ask you to send me money and I will print you a tribal card. You have paid for a piece of paper and nothing else.

Here is the sad part. There are many groups out there who are not state nor federally recognized that are indeed very genuine at heart. They may need some money to finance their affairs because they get no help from Uncle Sam. Because of the above example, they too have been labeled as wannabes, frauds, scam artists, and other names. Many of these groups contain some of the nicest, most sincere people that I have ever met. They are banded together as a group to stand proud of their heritage merely for the sake of that pride and nothing else. They don't have any benefits, they don't have state or federal recognition, and most do not have any assets, but they have heart. Most of these members will stand up for their heritage more proudly than anyone, but are still labeled. Here again, some bad seeds have helped ruin it for the rest. Will that ever change? Probably not.

Am I going to list a bunch of groups or tribes here that I think are right and a bunch whom I think are wrong? I feel that I would be asking for trouble if I did. Who am I to judge which groups may or may not be scams. They already know who they are. They know how to scam those who are wanting to be tribal members and be proud of their heritage. They know which types of people are more likely to come to them. If you are without tribal membership and you are seeking that, then do what you feel is right. You don't have to be a tribal member to be who you are or to be proud of your family. If it will help you to join a local group or tribe, then do it. Just be careful who you deal with.

So what is the moral of the story? If I earn the title wannabe or goof ball, then I will probably expect you to give it to me. If I show pride in my family and show respect to you for being what I consider part of that family, all I ask of you is respect for that. I don't care what tribe you belong to or what type of card you carry. I will be a friend to you all. I probably will never contact any of you and tell you that I am the only true medicine man, sent here by the ghost of a dead Chief. If I do, the number to my local mental institution, Broughton State Hospital, is in the book and I will need to go there. Try to respect those groups who are genuine in their efforts and pride as Indians who may not carry any type of card. If you run into frauds, that you know frauds and can prove the intent of criminal activity, then tell the right people. If I don't fit the profile of the whacked out wannabe, study about my heritage, show pride in it, and you still call me names, what am I to think of you? This is the story of me.

Conclusions

As I come to the conclusion of this book, I will briefly recount what has been said that I wish to remind you of. I could probably keep writing, but I feel that the included text is sufficient for now. I may seek to make a revised edition of this book, or write a new one with more information as I find it. Projects of this nature take time and when you have little of that, it takes even longer! Hopefully, it will be a reality and I would be proud if you would look for any future volumes that I write. I do this mainly for my family, but I made this book public for other's benefit if it has such a purpose. I also wanted the world to know that I am proud of who I am no matter how much ridicule that is received from such a pride. I get a great deal of flack about my interest in my Indian blood and people think I am crazy some times. Of course, these sort of responses come from non-Indian people or those who think little of such a thing. You will be surprised at the amount of people that think I am wasting my time and simply ask, "what do you get out of this?" That question is answered in this book on every page. I hold dear to me, things which others see as a waste of time. In this modern age, many of us have gotten to that point.

If you have learned anything from my writings, then I would hope that the above statement would be the main thing. We learn from our ancestors to love the land, protect the Earth Mother, and respect those who have gone on before us, while honoring their ways of life. Besides becoming culturally well rounded, I feel that this just shows that you have a good heart and that you can care about things other than this computer age. That could be what is wrong with many of our young people today that I deal with as a law enforcement officer.

I think that the problem lies within the parents not teaching them about what is important in life besides all of the "creature comforts." Sometimes a walk through the woods or an evening under the stars is much more relaxing and better for you than watching television or playing video games. These particular things are becoming more and more violent and I see it getting worse. I know that this is not a book on psychology or how to raise a child, but our ancestors can still teach us about family life today. Closeness of family and care for nature are two of those mighty lessons that we can still practice in our life times.

In this book, I included a section containing tips for researchers. I will always continue to search for more connections and it may take me a life time. I recommend that you do the same so that your children's children will not have to work so hard to find where they came from. I included sections on who I am and what a non-reservation mixed blood is like in my eyes. Many say that we are not the real Indians because of our mixed ancestry, but it still puzzles me who the real ones are. I don't think it is a matter of skin color, but a matter of what is in your heart and the loyalty that is displayed as a result of that loyalty.

In this book, I encouraged you to honor your ancestors in many ways, including researching your family tree and stories. Most family stories, by tradition, are not written down. There are reasons behind this, but you have to ask yourself if you can remember to pass them on or not. Some of the most trivial events in your life and the lives of your grand parents, may turn out to be some of the best memories to your children someday. I think that recording information about your family is a good idea. This acts as a record and also a notebook for those who want to learn about grand parents or great grand parents that they did not have the pleasure of meeting.

Many of my immediate relatives died before I was born, or before I was old enough to have an adult conversation with them. I hate that is the case, but there is nothing I can do to change it. My grandmother could have cleared up many of the mysteries that plagues me to this day. I was only 5 years old when she died and was not old enough to know to ask her these things. If your grand parents are still living, then you should be thankful and talk to them about things that you want to know. They are wiser than we are and have been around longer, but will not always be there. Cherish those days for they will one day be gone.

I also mentioned a few bits of history of the great Cherokee Nation and the persecution that they endured. I know that this was not a detailed history, nor was it all that there is. I wanted to stimulate your thinking and start a fire in your heart for your people. There are great lessons to be learned from them, but at the same time, a great sorrow in the air. Times were bad for the Cherokee during the old days and many tears fall today for those people who were involved.

By remembering these things with respect and honor, it helps you to better appreciate your family and your ties to the Cherokee people. You can't learn how to be Indian by reading a book, it has to be in your heart and be a lineage that comes from your elders. I have always had a special place in my heart for the Cherokee blood that runs in my family and always will. It has always been a comfortable thing for me to talk about in the family and makes me look at certain things differently than others. It is this part of you that proclaims that you are Indian. The color of your skin or the degree of blood is irrelevant in my opinion. That too can probably be argued, but it is how I feel.

There is so much more for me to learn about my people and the ways that helped them to survive to this day. I do not know it all and do not claim to know it all. I will never be able to say that I have all the knowledge that there is. Many things were lost and are not known, but I think that we will learn them again as if by an inner innate knowledge that will one day surface. It appears that I was the chosen one in my generation to pass the information on. I cannot explain why I do the things that I do, but I know that it just fell into place. I carry so many traits from grandpa Lambert, as well as his pride and other aspects that are not seen. It just appears that this is the way that it was meant to be. Knowing that, I have continued to work harder to find more about who I am and who my family was before me. It has taught me a great deal over the years and I cannot put it all into words. These feelings cannot be explained or defined, but can only be experienced.

I hope that you enjoyed this book and that it enlightened you on who I am. For my family, it is my hopes that this book filled many voids that may have been in your hearts. It may have answered some questions that you had and given you a direction to seek more. For the general public, I hope that you learned that I am a very proud person and openly speak of my ancestry. I hope that it showed you that there are still plenty of us mixed bloods who do care about that part of us called our Native American blood.

We care about the way things were and appreciate what the old ones did. We want to see positive changes for the Cherokee and be involved in that. We want the spirits of our ancestors to continue to live in our own actions and thinking. This book is only a part of that quest, but a very important part at that. It is not the entire story of my life and the lives of my ancestors, but only a glimpse into the deepest parts of our souls. So, if you ever get the feeling that the Cherokee or any other Native tribe are going away or being dissipated, think again. We are still here and will never leave. The sacred fire burns in my heart and thanks be to God for allowing it to warm my soul. This concludes this book, but is only the beginning of my path to find all there is to know about the great Cherokee Nation that I call family.

Glossary

Ani-Yunwiya In the Cherokee language, this means "the principal people."

Baker Roll This roll, taken in 1924, was the final roll of the Eastern Band of Cherokee Indians. Today, the current enrollment is registered on the Baker Roll Revised. Estimated enrolled members are about 12,000, most of whom live on the reservation in North Carolina.

BIA Acronym for the Bureau of Indian Affairs

CDIB Acronym for Certificate of Degree of Indian Blood

Cherokee Nation For the purpose of this text, this refers to the main body of Cherokee that currently reside in Oklahoma. They are sometimes referred to as the Cherokee Nation West. They number over 150,000 enrolled members. Both the Cherokee Nation West and the Eastern Band of Cherokee Indians are federally recognized.

Clans A clan is basically a unit within a tribe consisting of those that come from a common ancestor. Within the Cherokee Tribe, the person's clan membership is determined by their mother's clan affiliation. The Cherokee have seven clans, although originally there were more. In Cherokee culture, it was forbidden to marry within one's own clan. Clan members sought revenge against anyone who wronged another clan member. A clan can also be described as a large, but close family unit within a tribe. Most today do not know their clan affiliation, as no written records are known to exist of their memberships over the years. It was said by the Cherokee that one without a clan is basically not human and has no rights within the tribe. Obviously, that way of thinking had to change due to the broken matrilineal clan lines that have developed over the years.

Dawes Roll The Dawes roll is a government roll which basically divided up Indian lands in what is now Oklahoma among members of the Five Civilized tribes. Enrolled members had to meet certain requirements in order to be allotted land. The Dawes Act disbanded the tribes officially. Many refused to enroll, but some were forced to do so without their consent. The Keetowah Nighthawks, mostly full bloods, were most well known for refusing to enroll.

Disenfranchised In this book, the term refers to Cherokee or any other Native American that left the tribal domain and lost their citizenship. Although their legal citizenship was severed, their heritage remains the same. This also describes many Native Americans that do not show up on the government rolls. Also a controversial situation that many genealogists explain by stating that they were never Native American to begin with since they do not show up on the rolls.

Eastern Band Refers to the Cherokee who remained behind during the Trail of tears. Currently reside in the Great Smoky Mountains of North Carolina. This band is both federally and state recognized.

Federal Recognition This term, as used in this book, means that a particular tribe of Native Americans are recognized by the Federal Government as being a tribe. The Bureau of Indian Affairs, under the Department of the Interior, oversees many aspects of the tribe, mainly benefits or other government related affairs. For a tribe to meet the standards to become federally recognized, stringent requirements must be met and the tribe must petition the government for the same. For example, the group of people petitioning for federal recognition must show that they have lived together as a tribe, while maintaining aspects related to the same for a specific amount of time. Many other standards have to be met before federal recognition is extended.

Five Civilized Tribes Referring back to the Dawes Roll, this term makes reference to the Cherokee, Creek(Muskogee), Choctaw, Chickasaw, and Seminole.

Government Rolls This refers to rolls taken by various government officials in the past for the purpose of keeping account of the number of Native Americans in a given area, removal, or payment.

Qualla Boundary In essence, another word for the Cherokee Indian Reservation in North Carolina. Approximately 56,000 acres spread out in five counties. *See Eastern Band.*

Independent Tribes Across the US, there are numerous tribes, groups, organizations, etc. that are neither federally or state recognized. Often times, these groups are quite large in membership. These groups normally contain those individuals that do not meet the requirements for either type of recognition. Many of these groups are frowned upon by the recognized tribes and often labeled as wannabe Indians or scam artists. This has been proven most certainly to not always be the case. From the author's experience, many of these tribes contain some of the most genuine people that one could meet. As always, there are always exceptions. It is wise to investigate any group or tribe prior to enrollment in order to protect yourself from those that are out to defraud the public.

Indian Princess Theory Often heard during the course of Native American family research. Refers to those who state that their great grandmother, etc., was an Indian princess. It is a historical fact that there was never any such royalty within the Cherokee Nation. Often times, can mean that the female was the daughter of a chief or headman of the tribe. Most genealogists completely discount this theory when presented to them by clients; however there may be more truth to it than one may think. Keeping in mind that the term probably originated from one of European descent, whose only way of describing such a relationship would be to refer to royalty such as that of a King and his daughter.

Indian Removal Act This act was signed by President Andrew Jackson. It was carried out in 1838, when the Cherokee and others were rounded up forcibly and placed in removal forts. They then awaited the infamous journey to Indian Territory. The essence of this act was the fact that the discovery of gold in the land of the Cherokee created a greed in the white man's mind. The Indians were taken from their homes and lost their land which they loved so much. It was said that before they left on the long journey, some were seen kissing the ground and hugging the trees that stood on their beloved homelands.

Indian Territory This refers to what is now present day Oklahoma. Originally, it became the home of the Five Civilized Tribes, as well as others during the Indian Removal. The Dawes Commission allotted the lands to individuals that met the requirements, thus disbanding the tribal governments in the early 1900's. Today, Oklahoma is the home of the Cherokee Nation West.

John Ross As mentioned in this text, was principal chief of the Cherokee nation during the time period that included the trail of tears. Chief Ross was only about 1/8th Cherokee.

Junaluska A Cherokee chief that is buried in Robbinsville, NC. Junaluska saved the life of President Andrew Jackson during the battle of Horseshoe Bend against the Red Stick Creeks. Junaluska stated that had he known what Jackson was planning to do, he would have not only refused to save his life, but would have killed him himself.

Mixed Blood For the purpose of this text, this term refers to one who is of both Cherokee and white ancestry. Mixed blood individuals, in the past, were often listed on the federal census schedules as either white, mulatto, or Indian. Depending on their actual physical traits or the location in which they lived, many Cherokee were actually listed as white on the census schedules.

Old Settlers This refers to the group of Cherokees that moved west prior to the trail of tears. From about 1817-1828, they resided in Northwestern Arkansas. After that time period, they moved into Indian territory, which is now the state of Oklahoma.

Powwow A gathering of Native Americans, either one specific tribe or an inter-tribal affair, in which their ancestors are honored by dancing, singing, and story telling. Vendors sell their wares and food items. The powwow, although containing many traditional events, actually began in Oklahoma around 1900.

Sequoyah Inventor of the Cherokee alphabet or syllabary. Known to the whites as George Gist or Guess. Although Sequoyah could not read or write English, he developed the Cherokee alphabet and within a matter of months afterwards, the Cherokee people became a literate nation. Not long after the nation became accustomed to their written language, the first Cherokee newspaper was printed, the Cherokee Phoenix. Elias Boudinot was the editor of this paper.

State Recognition Similar in nature to federal recognition; however, the state in which the tribe resides oversees this action. Normally, the state will have an Indian affairs office that is in charge of tribal/state government relations. Tribes that are state recognized may receive benefits, but only from the state government. Often times, there are no benefits for members. Tribes are not automatically state recognized simply for existing within the boundaries of the state. Each state has it's own standards as to whom may be recognized and what benefits or assistance is available to those that are. Tribes that file as a tax exempt organization are not considered state recognized, unless the proper recognition has been extended by the state.

Trail of Tears This refers to the path taken during the execution of the Indian Removal Act in 1838-39. Thousands of Cherokee died along the way to Indian Territory. It is a fact that many avoided removal and some even escaped along the way to return to their homelands. No official records were kept of those that died, avoided the removal, or escaped. The trail of tears is known to be the greatest shame ever committed by the white man against the Native Americans. *See Indian Removal Act.*

Tsalagi Another word for the Cherokee in their own language. Is phonetically pronounced *jah lah ge* in the western dialect. The first syllable can also be pronounced with almost a *Z* sound, particularly in the East. It is important to note that there is a slight difference in the western and eastern dialects. Although each can understand the other without difficulty, the differences are noticeable. This change probably occurred in the western nation due to the removal and different areas that they lived.

Wannabe A term coined by modern day individuals which refers to a person who either wishes to be an Indian, but is not. Even some mixed bloods earn the title by being somewhat overzealous in their attempts to become acquainted with Native American culture should they have never been exposed to the same. Synonymous with *Twinkie*, another word with the same meaning often used by Native Americans to label the above types of individuals.

Bibliography

Blankenship, Bob *Cherokee Roots Volume One* Cherokee, NC: Bob Blankenship 11th Printing 1992

Cherokee, Indians of North America™ Video Collection Bala Cynwyd, PA: Schlessinger Video
Productions 1993

Eby, Richard & Howard, Gregg *Introduction to Cherokee* Fayetteville, Arkansas: VIP Publishing
Revised 1993

Finger, John, R. *The Eastern Band of Cherokees 1819-1900* Knoxville, Tennessee: The University of
Tennessee Press Second Printing 1994

Garrett, J.T. & Garrett, Michael *Medicine of the Cherokee: The Way of Right Relationship* Santa Fe,
New Mexico: Bear and Company Publishing 1996

Gormley, Myra, Vanderpool *Cherokee Connections* Baltimore, Maryland: Genealogical Publishing
Company 1995

Haithcock, Richard & Vickie *Southeastern Indian Refugees from Virginia, the Carolinas, and Tennessee*

In Ohio, Indiana, and Michigan Xenia, OH: Richard and Vickie Haithcock

Lakota Woman Atlanta, Georgia: Turner Home Entertainment VHS 1994

McClure, Tony Mack *Cherokee Proud* Somerville, Tennessee: Chunannee Books Second Edition 1999

Sharpe, J. Ed. *The Cherokees Past and Present* Cherokee, NC: Cherokee Publications, 1970

The Education of Little Tree Hollywood, California: Paramount Pictures VHS 1998

Tragedy and Triumph A Story of the Eastern Band of Cherokee Indians Charlotte, NC: Taylored Video
Services VHS

Voncannon, Brian, E. *Completing the Circle: The Hathcock Indian Blood* Locust, NC: Evening Storm
Enterprises Revised Edition 1999

About the Author

The author, Brian Voncannon was born near Charlotte, North Carolina He holds an associates degree in law enforcement technology, and has had two years of pre-med. study from Central Piedmont Community College in Charlotte. He is a veteran of the United States Army Reserve, with training as an infantry soldier and drill sergeant. His father is an enrolled member of the Appalachian American Indians of West Virginia. He and his mother are enrolled members of the Echota Cherokee Tribe of Alabama, which is one of seven recognized tribes in that state.

Brian recently published *Living Behind the Shield: A Modern Warrior's Path to Bravehood*, which gave an inside look at the law enforcement officer. Prior to that book, he self-published two other books. These publications entailed the story of his Native American heritage, as well as brief histories of the tribes involved. He is currently working on several other books on various topics. The author has found that writing has giving him a means to step aside from the stresses of everyday life. He plans to continue writing books and hopes to publish them all.